CHECKLIST OF EDITIONS OF GREEK AND LATIN PAPYRI, OSTRACA AND TABLETS
Fourth Edition

BULLETIN OF THE
AMERICAN SOCIETY OF PAPYROLOGISTS

SUPPLEMENTS

edited by
Ann Ellis Hanson

Number 7
CHECKLIST OF EDITIONS OF GREEK AND LATIN
PAPYRI, OSTRACA AND TABLETS
Fourth Edition
by
John F. Oates, Roger S. Bagnall,
William H. Willis, and Klaas A. Worp

CHECKLIST OF EDITIONS OF GREEK AND LATIN PAPYRI, OSTRACA AND TABLETS
Fourth Edition

JOHN F. OATES, ROGER S. BAGNALL, WILLIAM H. WILLIS, AND KLAAS A. WORP

Scholars Press
Atlanta, Georgia

CHECKLIST OF EDITIONS OF GREEK AND LATIN PAPYRI, OSTRACA AND TABLETS
Fourth Edition

John F. Oates, Roger S. Bagnall,
William H. Willis, and Klaas A. Worp

© 1992
The American Society of Papyrologists

Library of Congress Cataloging in Publication Data
Checklist of editions of Greek and Latin papyri, ostraca and tablets/
by John F. Oates ... [et al.]. — 4th ed.
    p. cm. — (Bulletin of the American Society of Papyrologists.
Supplements; no. 7)
    ISBN 1-55540-782-X (alk. paper)
    1. Manuscripts, Classical (Papyri)—Bibliography. 2. Tablets
(Paleography)—Bibliography. 3. Ostraka—Bibliography.   I. Oates,
John F.   II. Series.
Z6604.C47   1992
016.481'1—dc20   92-33810
                                                      CIP

Printed in the United States of America
on acid-free paper
∞

CONTENTS

PREFACE

The primary purpose of the *Checklist of Editions of Greek and Latin Papyri, Ostraca and Tablets* is to provide for scholars and librarians a ready bibliography of all monographic volumes, both current and out-of-print, of texts written on papyrus, parchment, ostraca or wood tablets. Texts published in periodicals as journal articles are normally excluded, since they are regularly republished in successive volumes of *Sammelbuch Griechischer Urkunden aus Ägypten*, the volumes of which are included; but groups of texts published in journals if furnished with full indices are classed as independent monographic publications and so are included. Many volumes containing documentary texts publish literary and subliterary texts as well, and such volumes are of course included, together with volumes of the same series that are exclusively literary. But we have made no systematic attempt to include *all* exclusively literary and subliterary volumes, since these are fully catalogued in Roger A. Pack, *The Greek and Latin Literary Texts from Greco-Roman Egypt*, ed. 2 (Ann Arbor 1965), and in the forthcoming *Catalogue des papyrus littéraires grecs et latins* (Mertens-Pack[3]) by Paul Mertens. Similarly, Jewish and Christian literary and subliterary texts may be found in J. van Haelst, *Catalogue des papyrus littéraires juifs et chrétiens* (Paris 1976).

A second objective of the *Checklist* is to establish a standard list of abbreviations of papyrological volumes, as commissioned by a committee of the XIII International Congress of Papyrology meeting at Marburg in 1971. Brevity and clarity, not rigid consistency, have been the chief goals in choosing abbreviations, based on the following principles in order of priority: first, the site of the collection (e.g. *P.Mich., O.Mich.*); second, the find-site (*P.Oxy., T.Vindol.*); third, in the case of an archive, the name of the person or group whose papers constitute the archive (*P.Petaus*); if none of these is feasible, fourth, the owner of the collection (*P.Mert.*) or honorand of a volume from various sources (*P.Coll. Youtie, P.Turner*); or finally, the editor (*P.Meyer*). Exceptions have been allowed only in some cases of long sanctioned usage (*BGU, CPR, UPZ, Stud.Pal., SB*). The system of citation established by the *Checklist* has been adopted by the American Society of Papyrologists as official for their publications and by a number of other scholarly journals.

The third function of the *Checklist* is to provide a canon of the volumes containing documentary texts which have been or will be entered in the Duke Data Bank of Documentary Papyri, in order that a complete corpus of all published Greek and Latin documentary papyri, ostraca and tablets in machine readable form may easily be accessed, searched and concordanced by computer. Each volume already entered in the Data Bank is starred with an asterisk. Of the 440 volumes published to date, 375 are available on PHI CD ROM no. 6 issued by the Packard Humanities Institute, including all texts entered into the Data Bank up to 5 April 1991. Data entry continues, and additional volumes are being entered continuously in inverse order of their date of publication, with priority given to those published most recently. Volumes entered since 5 April 1991 are also asterisked in the *Checklist*; they, and the entire Data Bank, are available on magnetic tape at cost from the Duke Data Bank.

The present edition of the *Checklist* has been extensively revised and corrected as of August, 1992. Preceding it in printed form were the Third Edition, closed in November 1984 (*BASP* Supplement No. 4, 1985); the Second Edition, closed on 30 June 1978 (*BASP* Supplement No. 1, 1978); and the First Edition, published as *BASP* XI no. 1 (1974). For an account of the origin and development of the *Checklist*, the reader is referred to the succession of Prefaces printed in the Third Edition, pp. vii-xiii.

The basic data for the *Checklist* are maintained in a continually updated version at the Duke Data Bank. PHI CD ROM no. 6 contains Electronic Edition B as it stood on 5 April 1991. Electronic Edition A, revised as of 8 September 1988, was included on PHI CD ROM no. 2.

I. PAPYRI

*All documentary texts in volumes marked by an asterisk have been entered in the Duke Data Bank of Documentary Papyri and are available for search by computer. A parenthesized asterisk indicates that all documentary volumes of a series have been entered or that an earlier edition has been replaced by a later one which has been entered. See Section VII for the information on availability provided in square brackets.

(*)Actenstücke = *Actenstücke aus der königlichen Bank zu Theben in den Museen zu Berlin, London, Paris*, ed. U. Wilcken. Berlin 1887. Nos. 1-12. (*AbhBerlin* 1886, Anhang, Abh.1; rp. in U. Wilcken, *Berliner Akademieschriften zur Alten Geschichte und Papyruskunde* I [Leipzig 1970] 39-104). Republished in *UPZ* *II 205-207, 214-215, 217-221, 226-228. [MF 1.10; rp. ZA]

BGU = *Aegyptische Urkunden aus den Königlichen* (later *Staatlichen*) *Museen zu Berlin, Griechische Urkunden*. Berlin.

    I, 1895. Nos. 1-361. [MF 1.1; rp. CG]

    II, 1898. Nos. 362-696. [MF 1.2; rp. CG]

    III, 1903. Nos. 697-1012. [MF 1.3; rp. CG]

    *IV, 1912. Nos. 1013-1209. [MF 1.4; rp. CG]

    *V, *Der Gnomon des Idios Logos*. Erster Teil: *Der Text*, ed. W. Schubart. 1919. Zweiter Teil: *Das Kommentar*, by W. Graf von Uxkull Gyllenband. 1934. No. 1210. [MF 1.5; rp. CG]

    *VI, *Papyri und Ostraka der Ptolemäerzeit*, ed. W. Schubart, E. Kühn. 1922. Nos. 1211-1303 are papyri; nos. 1304-1499 are ostraca. [MF 1.6; rp. CG]

    *VII, *Papyri, Ostraka und Wachstafeln aus Philadelphia im Fayûm*, ed. P. Viereck and F. Zucker. 1926. Nos. 1563-1689 are papyri; nos. 1500-1565, 1697-1729 are ostraca; nos. 1690-1696 wooden tablets. [MF 1.7; rp. CG]

    *VIII, *Spätptolemäische Papyri aus amtlichen Büros des Herakleopolites*, ed. W. Schubart and D. Schäfer. 1933. Nos. 1730-1890. [MF 1.8; rp. CG]

*IX, *Steuerlisten römischer Zeit aus Theadelphia*, ed. H. Kortenbeutel. 1937. Nos. 1891-1900. [MF 1.9; rp. CG]

*X, *Papyrusurkunden aus ptolemäischer Zeit*, ed. W. Müller. 1970. Nos. 1901-2011. [o.e. AV]

*XI, *Urkunden römischer Zeit*, ed. H. Maehler. Part I, 1966; Part II, 1968. Nos. 2012-2131. [o.e. BAM]

*XII, *Papyri aus Hermupolis*, ed. H. Maehler. 1974. Nos. 2132-2210. [o.e. BAM]

*XIII, *Greek Papyri from Roman Egypt*, ed. W.M. Brashear. 1976. Nos. 2211-2366. [o.e. BAM]

*XIV, *Ptolemäische Urkunden aus Mumienkartonage*, ed. W.M. Brashear. 1980. Nos. 2367-2450 are papyri; nos. 2451-2457 ostraca. [o.e. BAM]

*XV, *Financial and Administrative Documents from Roman Egypt*, ed. C.A. Nelson. 1983. Nos. 2458-2557. [o.e. BAM]

BKT = *Berliner Klassikertexte*. Berlin.

I, *Didymos, Kommentar zu Demosthenes (Papyrus 9780) nebst Wörterbuch zu Demosthenes' Aristocratea (Papyrus 5008)*, ed. H. Diels and W. Schubart. 1904. [MF 1.11]

II, *Anonymer Kommentar zu Platons Theaetet (Papyrus 9782) nebst drei Bruchstücken philosophischen Inhalts (Pap. N.8; P.9766. 9569)*, ed. H. Diels and W. Schubart. 1905. [MF 1.12]

III, *Griechische Papyri medizinischen und naturwissenschaftlichen Inhalts*, ed. K. Kalbfleisch and H. Schöne. 1905. [MF 1.13]

IV, *Hierokles ethische Elementarlehre (Papyrus 9780), nebst den bei Stobäus erhaltenen ethischen Exzerpten aus Hierokles*, ed. H. von Arnim. 1906. [MF 1.14]

V, *Griechische Dichterfragmente*: Part I, *Epische und elegische Fragmente*; Part II, *Lyrische und dramatische Fragmente*, ed. W. Schubart and U. von Wilamowitz-Moellendorff. 1907. [MF 1.15]

VI, *Altchristliche Texte*, ed. C. Schmidt, W. Schubart. 1910. [MF 1.16]

VII, *Rhetorische Papyri*, ed. K. Kunst. 1923. [MF 1.17]

VIII, *Berliner Septuagintafragmente*, ed. O. Stegmüller. 1939. [MF 1.18]

CPR = *Corpus Papyrorum Raineri*. Vienna.

I, *Griechische Texte I, Rechtsurkunden*, ed. C. Wessely. 1895. Nos. 1-247. [MF 1.85; rp. CG]

II, *Koptische Texte*, ed. J. Krall. 1895. Nos. 1-255. [MF 2.67] Many texts are reedited in *CPR* IV; see concordance there p. xv.

III, *Series Arabica* I, Part 1, *Allgemeine Einführung in die arabischen Papyri*; Part 2, *Protokolle*, Nos. 1-377; Part 3, Plates, ed. A. Grohmann. 1924.

IV, *Die koptischen Rechtsurkunden der Papyrussammlung der Oesterreichischen Nationalbibliothek*, ed. W. Till. 1958. Nos. 1-212. [o.e. ÖNB]

*V, *Griechische Texte* II, ed. J.R. Rea and P.J. Sijpesteijn. 1976. Nos. 1-25 plus P.Vindob. G 39847 (No. 26). [o.e. ÖNB]

*VI.1, *Griechische Texte* III, Part 1, ed. H. Harrauer and S.M.E. van Lith. Nos. 1-71; separate fascicle of plates. 1978. [o.e. ÖNB]

*VI.2, *Griechische Texte* III, Part 2, ed. H. Harrauer. Nos. 72-85; separate fascicle of plates. 1985. [o.e. ÖNB]

*VII, *Griechische Texte* IV, ed. H. Zilliacus, J. Frösén, P. Hohti, J. Kaimio, M. Kaimio. 1979. Nos. 1-60; separate fascicle of plates. [o.e. ÖNB]

*VIII, *Griechische Texte* V, ed. P.J. Sijpesteijn and K.A. Worp. 1983. Nos. 1-85; separate fascicle of plates. [o.e. ÖNB]

*IX, *Griechische Texte* VI, ed. Joh.M. Diethart. Part 1, 1984. Nos. 1-79; separate fascicle of plates. [o.e. ÖNB]

*X, *Griechische Texte* VII, ed. H. Harrauer et alii. 1986. Nos. 1-140; nos. 32-34 are ostraca; separate fascicle of plates. [o.e. ÖNB]

XI, Not yet published

XII, *Koptische Texte*, ed. Monika R.M. Hasitzka. 1987. Nos. 1-38; separate fascicle of plates. [o.e. ÖNB]

*XIII, *Griechische Texte* IX, ed. H. Harrauer. 1987. Nos. 1-31; separate fascicle of plates. [o.e. ÖNB]

*XIV, *Griechische Texte* X, *Greek Papyri of the Byzantine Period*, ed. G. Fantoni. 1989. Nos. 1-55; separate fascicle of plates. [o.e. ÖNB]

*XV, *Griechische Texte* XI, *Papiri greci di Socnopaiu Nesos e dell'Arsinoites*, ed. G. Messeri Savorelli. 1990. Nos. 1-53; separate fascicle of plates. [o.e. ÖNB]

XVI, not yet published

*XVIIA, *Griechische Texte* XIIA, *Die Archive der Aurelii Adelphios und Asklepiades*, ed. K.A. Worp. 1991. Nos. 1-39 and App. a-c; separate fascicle of plates. [o.e. ÖNB]

*XVIIB, *Griechische Texte* XIIB, *Papyri aus Panopolis*, ed. P.J. Sijpesteijn. 1991. Nos. 1-47; separate fascicle of plates. [o.e. ÖNB]

XVIII, *Griechische Texte* XIII, *Das Vertragsregister von Theogenis (P.Vindob. G 40618)*, ed. B. Kramer. 1991. Nos. 1-34; separate fascicle of plates. [o.e. ÖNB]

*P.Aberd. = *Catalogue of Greek and Latin Papyri and Ostraca in the Possession of the University of Aberdeen*, ed. E.G. Turner. Aberdeen 1939. (Aberdeen Univ. Studies 116). Nos. 1-2, 7-72, 104-197 are papyri; nos. 3-6, 73-103 are ostraca. [MF 2.104]

*P.Abinn. = *The Abinnaeus Archive: Papers of a Roman Officer in the Reign of Constantius II*, ed. H.I. Bell, V. Martin, E.G. Turner, D. van Berchem. Oxford 1962. Nos. 1-82. [Rp. CG] See also *SB* X 10755 and XIV 11380.

*P.Achm. = *Les Papyrus grecs d'Achmîm à la Bibliothèque Nationale de Paris*, ed. P. Collart. Cairo 1930. (*BIFAO* 31 [1930] 33-111). Nos. 1-9. [MF 1.73]

*P.Adl. = *The Adler Papyri*, Greek texts ed. E.N. Adler, J.G. Tait, F.M. Heichelheim. Demotic Texts ed. F.Ll. Griffith. Oxford 1939. Greek nos. 1-21, Demotic nos. 1-30. [Rp. CG]

*P.Alex. = *Papyrus grecs du Musée Gréco-Romain d'Alexandrie*, ed. A. Swiderek and M. Vandoni. Warsaw 1964. (Polska Akademia Nauk. Zaklad Archeologii Sródziemnomorskiej, Prace 2. Travaux du Centre d'Archéologie Méditerranéenne de l'Académie Polonaise des Sciences). Nos. 1-40 on pp.47-79; otherwise a catalogue of descriptions and other material relating to the Alexandria papyri. [o.p.]

*P.Alex.Giss. = *Papyri variae Alexandrinae et Gissenses*, ed. J. Schwartz. Brussels 1969. (Pap.Brux. VII). Texts reprinted as *SB* X 10617-10653. Nos. 1-61; nos. 62-73 are notes to other texts. [o.e. FERE]

P.Amh. = *The Amherst Papyri, Being an Account of the Greek Papyri in the Collection of the Right Hon. Lord Amherst of Hackney, F.S.A. at Didlington Hall, Norfolk*, ed. B.P. Grenfell and A.S. Hunt. London.

  I, *The Ascension of Isaiah and Other Theological Fragments*. 1900. Nos. 1-9. [MF 1.43; rp. CG]

  II, *Classical Fragments and Documents of the Ptolemaic, Roman and Byzantine Periods*. 1901. Nos. 10-201. [MF 1.44; rp. CG]

*P.Amst. I = *Die Amsterdamer Papyri* I, ed. R.P. Salomons, P.J. Sijpesteijn, K.A. Worp. Zutphen 1980. (Stud.Amst. XIV). Nos. 1-100. [o.e. TPC] Cf. also *P.Gron.Amst.*

*P.Anag. = *Corpus Papyrorum Anagennesis*, ed. F. Farid. Athens 1986. Revised texts originally published by various editors in the journal *Anagennesis* vols. 1-3 (1981-1983).

(*)P.Ant. = *The Antinoopolis Papyri*. London.
 *I, ed. C.H. Roberts. 1950. (Egypt Exploration Society, Graeco-Roman Memoirs 28). Nos. 7-50. (For nos. 1-6 see III, Corpora, *Shorthand Manuals*). [o.e. EES]
 *II, ed. J.W.B. Barns and H. Zilliacus. 1960. (Egypt Exploration Society, Graeco-Roman Memoirs 37). Nos. 51-110. [o.e. EES]
 *III, ed. J.W.B. Barns and H. Zilliacus. 1967. (Egypt Exploration Society, Graeco-Roman Memoirs 47). Nos. 111-214. [o.e. EES]

*P.Apoll. = *Papyrus grecs d'Apollônos Anô*, ed. R. Rémondon. Cairo 1953. Nos. 1-105. (Documents de fouilles de l'Institut Français d'Archéologie Orientale du Caire 19). [MF 1.41] Nos. 106 and 107 = *SB* XIV 11917-11918; nos. 108-110 = *SB* XVI 12428-12431.

*P.Ashm. = "Greek Documents and Subscriptions," ed. J.W.B. Barns, in E.A.E. Reymond, *Catalogue of Demotic Papyri in the Ashmolean Museum* I. Oxford 1973. Nos. 22-25 are Greek subscriptions of Demotic documents. Greek texts reprinted as *SB* XIV 11404-11413. A further text is published at *SB* I 4369. [o.e. OUP]

*P.Athen. = *Papyri Societatis Archaeologicae Atheniensis*, ed. G.A. Petropoulos. Athens 1939. (Πραγματεῖαι τῆς ᾿Ακαδημίας ᾿Αθηνῶν 10). Nos. 1-70. [MF 1.64; rp. CG]. Further texts published in ᾿Ανέκδοτοι φιλολογικοὶ καὶ ἰδιωτικοὶ πάπυροι, ed. M.G. Tsoukalas. Athens 1962. (Βιβλιοθήκη τῆς ἐν ᾿Αθήναις Φιλεκπαιδευτικῆς ῾Εταιρείας 17). The documents are reprinted in *SB* VIII 9860-62.

*P.Babatha = *The Documents from the Bar Kochba Period in the Cave of Letters: Greek Papyri*, ed. N. Lewis. Jerusalem 1989. This volume contains the Greek texts of the archive, nos. 5, 11-35 and 37, with their Aramaic and Nabataean subscriptions. A separate volume will publish the Aramaic and Nabataean texts of the archive, nos. 1-4, 6-10 and 36. [o.e. Israel Exploration Society]

*P.Bacch. = "The Archives of the Temple of Soknobraisis at Bacchias," ed. E.H. Gilliam, in *YCS* 10 (1947) 179-281. Nos. 1-25. Texts reprinted as *SB* VI 9319-9339. See also *P.Lund* IV. [MF 2.77]

(*)P.Bad. = *Veröffentlichungen aus den badischen Papyrus Sammlungen.*
Heidelberg. Series continues with *P.Heid.* I = N.F. II.
I, *Demotische Papyri*, ed. W. Spiegelberg. 1923. [MF 2.49]
*II, *Griechische Papyri*, ed. F. Bilabel. 1923. Nos. 1-45. [MF 2.50]
III, *Ein koptisches Fragment über die Begründer des Manichäismus*, ed.
F. Bilabel. 1924. No. 46. [MF 2.51]
*IV, *Griechische Papyri*, ed. F. Bilabel. 1924. Nos. 47-59, 70-97 are
papyri, 98-110 ostraca, 60-65 and 111 tablets, 66-69 pots. [MF
2.52]
V, *Griechische, koptische und arabische Texte zur Religion und
religiösen Literatur in Aegyptens Spätzeit*, ed. F. Bilabel and A.
Grohmann. 1934. Nos. 112-167. [MF 2.53]
*VI, *Griechische Papyri*, ed. G.A. Gerhard. 1938. Nos. 168-180. [MF
2.54]. Numbering continued in *P.Heid.* I = N.F. II.
*P.Bal. = *Bala'izah: Coptic Texts from Deir el Bala'izah in Upper Egypt*,
ed. P.E. Kahle, 2 vols., London 1954. The following texts are
Greek in whole or part: I 2 (parchment), 29; II 123, 130, 148,
180-82, 203-204, 286-89, 296-300, 308, 315, 345-46, 355-56, 361,
374-375, 381, 383, 386-394, 408 (papyri). [o.p.]
*P.Bas. = *Papyrusurkunden der öffentlichen Bibliothek der Universität zu
Basel*: Pt. I, *Urkunden in griechischer Sprache*, ed. E. Rabel. Nos.
1-26. Pt. II, *Ein koptischer Vertrag*, ed. W. Spiegelberg. Berlin
1917. (AbhGöttingen N.F. 16.3). [Rp. V&R; MF 1.86]
*P.Batav. = *Textes grecs, démotiques et bilingues*, ed. E. Boswinkel and
P.W. Pestman. Leiden 1978. (Pap.Lugd.Bat. XIX). Nos. 1-2, 26-
28, 42-48 Demotic; 3, 5, 25, 29-32, 40-41 bilingual (Greek and
Demotic); 4, 6-24, 33-39 Greek. Nos. 1-24 are papyri; 25-28
ostraca; 29-39 linen; 40-48 mummy labels. [o.e. EJB]
P.Beatty = *Chester Beatty Biblical Papyri*, ed. F.G. Kenyon. London. [I-
VIII, MF 1.84]
I, *General Introduction*. 1933. [o.e. HF]
II, *The Gospels and Acts*. 1933. Pt. 2, Plates. 1934. [text o.e. HF]
III, *Pauline Epistles and Revelation*. 1934. Pt. 2, Plates of *Revelation*.
1936. [o.e. HF]
Suppl. *Pauline Epistles*. 1936. Plates, 1937. [o.e. HF]
IV, *Genesis*. 1934. Pt. 2, *Genesis (Pap. IV)* Plates. 1935. Pt. 3, *Genesis
(Pap. IV)* Plates. 1936. [o.e. HF]
V, *Numbers and Deuteronomy*. 1935. [o.e. HF]
VI, *Isaiah, Jeremiah, Ecclesiasticus*. 1937. [o.e. HF]

V and VI, Plates. 1958. [o.e. HF]

VII, *Ezekiel, Daniel, Esther.* 1937. Pt. 2, Plates. 1938. [o.e. HF]

VIII, *Enoch and Melito.* Plates, 1941. Texts published in *The Last Chapters of Enoch in Greek,* ed. C. Bonner with the collaboration of H.C. Youtie. London 1937. (Studies and Documents VIII). [plates o.e. HF]

P.Berl.Bibl. = *Frammenti di papiri greci asservati nella Reale Biblioteca di Berlino,* ed. G. Parthey. 1865 (Memorie dell'Istituto di Correspondenza Archeologica 2 [1865] 438-462). Cf. *SB* II p. 114.

*P.Berl.Bork. = *Une description topographique des immeubles à Panopolis,* ed. Z. Borkowski. Warsaw 1975. [o.e. AP]

*P.Berl.Brash. = *Select Papyri from West Berlin,* ed. W.M. Brashear. Diss. Ann Arbor 1973, order no. 73-24,529. Of the 19 texts all are reedited in *BGU* XIII or XIV or as *SB* XIV 11855 and 11856. No. 2 is again reedited as *P.Gen.* II 103, no. 8 as *C.Pap.Gr.* II 43. There is a concordance at *SB* XIV 11855.

*P.Berl.Frisk = *Bankakten aus dem Faijûm nebst anderen Berliner Papyri,* ed. H. Frisk. Gothenburg 1931. (Göteborgs kungl. Vetenskaps och Vitterhets-Samhälles Handlingar, Femte Följden, Ser. A,2,2). Nos. 1-6. Texts reprinted as *SB* V 7515-7520. [MF 2.34; rp. CG]

(*)P.Berl.Leihg. = *Berliner Leihgabe griechischer Papyri.*

*I, ed. T. Kalén and the Greek Seminar at Uppsala. Uppsala 1932. (Uppsala Universitets Årsskrift 1932, Filosofi, Språkvetenskap och Historiska Vetenskaper 1). Nos. 1-25. [MF 1.61]

*II, aus dem Nachlass T. Kaléns ed. A. Tomsin. Uppsala 1977. (Studia Graeca Upsaliensia XII). Nos. 26-46. [o.e. AW]

*P.Berl.Möller = *Griechische Papyri aus dem Berliner Museum,* ed. S. Möller. Gothenburg 1929. Nos. 1-13. Texts reprinted as *SB* IV 7338-7350. [MF 2.87]

(*)P.Berl.Schmidt = *Die griechischen Papyrusurkunden der Königlichen Bibliothek zu Berlin,* ed. W.A. Schmidt. Berlin 1842. (Forschungen auf dem Gebiete des Altertums 1). Nos. 1-2. Texts reprinted *SB* I 4503-4504.

(*)P.Berl.Thun. = *Sitologen-Papyri aus dem Berliner Museum,* ed. K. Thunell. Uppsala 1924. Texts reprinted as *SB* III 7193-7196 and as *P.Berl.Leihg.* I 1-4. [MF 2.106; rp.CG]

*P.Berl.Zill. = *Vierzehn Berliner griechische Papyri*, ed. H. Zilliacus. Helsingfors 1941. (Societas Scientiarum Fennica, Commentationes Humanarum Litterarum XI,4). Nos. 1-14. [MF 1.32]

P.Bodm. = *Papyrus Bodmer*, publications of Bibliotheca Bodmeriana, Cologny-Génève (unless otherwise stated), as follows:

I, *Iliade, chants 5 et 6*, ed. V. Martin. 1954. [o.p.]

II, *Évangile de Jean (chaps. 1-14)*, ed. V. Martin. 1956. With supplement, chaps. 14-21, ed. V. Martin. 1958. New edition, ed. V. Martin and J.W.B. Barns. 1962. With photographic reproduction of complete text of chaps. 1-21. [new ed. o.e. BB]

III, *Évangile de Jean et Genèse I IV, 2 en bohaïrique*, ed. R. Kasser. Louvain 1958. (Corpus Scriptorum Christianorum Orientalium, vols. 177, 178 = Scriptores Coptici, vols. 25, 26).

IV, *Ménandre: Le Dyscolos*, ed. V. Martin. 1958. [o.p.]

V, *Nativité de Marie*, ed. M. Testuz. 1958. [o.p.]

VI, *Livre des Proverbes* (Coptic), ed. R. Kasser. Louvain 1960. (Corpus Scriptorum Christianorum Orientalium, vols. 194, 195 = Scriptores Coptici, vols. 27, 28).

VII-IX, *L'épître de Jude, les deux épîtres de Pierre, les Psaumes 33 et 34*, ed. M. Testuz. 1959. [o.p.]

X-XII: X, *Correspondance apocryphe des Corinthiens et de l'apôtre Paul*; XI, *Onzième Ode de Salomon*; XII, *Fragment d'un hymne liturgique*, ed. M. Testuz. 1959. [o.p.]

XIII, *Homélie sur la Pâque par Méliton de Sardes*, ed. M. Testuz. 1960. [o.p.]

XIV-XV, *Évangile de Luc chap. 3-24, Évangile de Jean chap. 1-15*, ed. V. Martin and R. Kasser. 1961. [o.e. BB]

XVI, *Exode I XV, 21 en sahidique*, ed. R. Kasser. 1961. [o.p.]

XVII, *Actes des Apôtres, Épîtres de Jacques, Pierre, Jean et Jude*, ed. R. Kasser. 1961. [o.p.]

XVIII, *Deutéronome I X, 7 en sahidique*, ed. R. Kasser. 1962. [o.p.]

XIX, *Évangile de Matthieu XIV, 28-XXVIII, 20; Épître aux Romains I,1-II,3 en sahidique*, ed. R. Kasser. 1962. [o.e. BB]

XX, *Apologie de Philéas, évêque de Thmouis*, ed. V. Martin. 1964. [o.e. BB]

XXI, *Josué VI,16-25, VII,6-XI,23, XXII,1-2, 19-XXIII,7, 15-XXIV,23 en sahidique*, ed. R. Kasser. 1963. [o.e. BB]

XXII, *Jérémie XL,3-LII,34; Lamentations; Épître de Jérémie; Baruch I, 1-V,5 en sahidique* (includes Mississippi Coptic Codex II), ed. R. Kasser. 1964. [o.e. BB]

XXIII, *Esaïe, XLVII,1-LXVI,24 en sahidique*, ed. R. Kasser. 1965. [o.e. BB]

XXIV, *Psaumes XVII-CXVIII*, ed. R. Kasser and M. Testuz. 1967. [o.e. BB]

XXV, *Ménandre: La Samienne*, ed. R. Kasser with the collaboration of C. Austin. 1969. [o.e. BB]

XXVI, *Ménandre: Le Bouclier*, ed. R. Kasser with the collaboration of C. Austin. 1969. [with XXV].

XXVII, "Il papiro di Tucidide della Bibliotheca Bodmeriana (P.Bodmer XXVII)," ed. A. Carlini, *MusHelv* 32 (1975) 33-40.

XXVIII, "Papyrus Bodmer XXVIII: A Satyr Play on the Confrontation of Heracles and Atlas," ed. E.G. Turner, *MusHelv* 33 (1976) 1-23.

XXIX, *Vision de Dorothéos*, ed. A. Hurst, O. Reverdin, J. Rudhardt, with an appendix by R. Kasser and G. Cavallo describing and dating the "Codex des Visions." 1984. [o.e. BB]

XXXVIII, *Erma: Il Pastore (Ia-IIIa visione)*, ed. A. Carlini with collaboration of L. Giaccone, and with an appendix by R. Kasser, G. Cavallo and J. van Haelst, "Nouvelle description du Codex des Visions." 1991. [o.e. BB]

XLV and XLVI, "Susanna e la prima visione di Daniele in due papiri inediti della Bibliotheca Bodmeriana: P.Bodm. XLV et P.Bodm. XLVI," ed. A. Carlini and A. Citi, *MusHelv* 38 (1981) 81-120.

XLVIII, "Papyrus Bodmer 48 (Iliade 1.45-58)," ed. A. Hurst, *MusHelv* 47 (1990) 30-33.

XLIX, "Papyrus Bodmer 49 (Odyssee 9.455-488 et 526-556; 10.188-215)," ed. A. Hurst, *MusHelv* 43 (1986) 221-30.

L, "Papyrus Bodmer L. Das neutestamentliche Papyrusfragment P73 = Mt. 25,43 / 26,2-3," ed. C.P. Theide, *MusHelv* 47 (1990) 35-40.

*P.Bon. = *Papyri Bononienses*, ed. O. Montevecchi. Milan 1953. (Pubblicazioni dell'Università Cattolica del Sacro Cuore, N.S. 42). Nos. 1-49; no. 50 contains a mummy ticket and a parchment. [o.e. VP]

*P.Bour. = *Les Papyrus Bouriant*, ed. P. Collart. Paris 1926. Nos. 1-63. [MF 1.87]

*P.Brem. = *Die Bremer Papyri*, ed. U. Wilcken. Berlin 1936. (*AbhBerlin* 1936,2). Nos. 1-83 Greek; no. 84 Coptic. Rp. in U. Wilcken, *Berliner Akademieschriften zur alten Geschichte und Papyruskunde* II, pp.193-368. Leipzig 1970. [Rp. ZA; MF 1.83]

P.Brook. = *Greek and Latin Papyri, Ostraca, and Wooden Tablets in the Collection of the Brooklyn Museum*, ed. J.C. Shelton. Florence 1992. (Pap.Flor. XXII). Nos. 1-26 and 88-91 are papyri; nos. 27-31 tablets; nos. 32-87 ostraca; nos. 92-115 descriptions of papyri; nos. 116-184 descriptions of ostraca. Nos. 24, 100, and 101 are Latin; no. 20 is bilingual. [o.e. LGF]

*P.Brux. = *Papyri Bruxellenses Graecae* I, ed. G. Nachtergael. Brussels 1974. Nos. 1-21. Nos. 1-18 are a republication of *P.Brux.inv.* E 7616. See Pap.Lugd.Bat. V. [o.e. FERE]

    II, *Le poème élégiaque hellénistique P. Brux. Inv. E. 8934 et P. Sorb. Inv. 2254. Édition, commentaire et analyse stylistique*, ed. M. Huys. 1991. No. 22. [o.e. FERE]

*P.Bub. = *Die verkohlten Papyri aus Bubastos*, Opladen.

    *I, Rolls 1-4, ed. J. Frösén and D. Hagedorn. 1990. (Pap.Colon. XV, Bd. 1). [o.e. WDV]

P.Cair.Cat. = *Greek Papyri, Catalogue général des antiquités égyptiennes du Musée du Caire*, Nos. 10001-10869, ed. B.P. Grenfell and A.S. Hunt. Oxford 1903. Not a publication of papyri, but a list and short description of papyri in the Cairo Museum. Texts are given only for Nos. 10696, 10735, and 10736. A concordance between inventory numbers and later publications is given by K.A. Worp, *ZPE* 91 (1992) 95-98. [MF 2.30; rp. AMH, OZ]

P.Cair.Goodsp. = *Greek Papyri from the Cairo Museum*, ed. E.J. Goodspeed. Chicago 1902. (University of Chicago, Decennial Publications, from vol. V). Includes twelve papyri from the collection of the Rev. J.R. Alexander (now in the collection of Westminster College) and three of Goodspeed's; all are numbered consecutively. Nos. 1-30. [MF 2.27; rp. CG] See also *P.Chic.* and *P.Kar.Goodsp.* For the Goodspeed papyrus collection see *ZPE* 16 (1975) 27-32.

*P.Cair.Isid. = *The Archive of Aurelius Isidorus in the Egyptian Museum, Cairo, and the University of Michigan*, ed. A.E.R. Boak and H.C. Youtie. Ann Arbor 1960. Nos. 1-146. [MF 1.28]

(*)P.Cair.Masp. = *Papyrus grecs d'époque byzantine, Catalogue général des antiquités égyptiennes du Musée du Caire*, ed. J. Maspero. Cairo.

    *I, (Cat. Vol. 51), 1911. Nos. 67001-67124. [MF 1.38; rp. OZ/CG]

    *II, (Cat. Vol. 54), 1913. Nos. 67125-67278. An expanded and corrected text of no. 67140 is republished in vol. III pp.1-2; the subsequently discovered first part of no. 67169 is published as no. 67169bis in vol. III pp.2-6. [MF 1.39; rp. OZ/CG]

*III, (Cat. Vol. 73), 1916. Nos. 67279-67359. [MF 1.40; rp. OZ/CG]

*P.Cair.Mich. = *A Tax List from Karanis (P.Cair.Mich. 359).* Part 1, *The Text,* ed. H. Riad and J.C. Shelton; Part 2, *Commentary and Indexes,* ed. J. C. Shelton. Bonn 1975-1977. (Pap.Texte Abh. XVII-XVIII). [o.e. RH]

*P.Cair.Preis. = *Griechische Urkunden des Aegyptischen Museums zu Kairo,* ed. F. Preisigke. Strassburg 1911. (Schriften d. Wiss. Gesellschaft zu Strassburg 8). Nos. 1-48. [MF 2.68]

(*)P.Cair.Zen. = *Zenon Papyri, Catalogue général des antiquités égyptiennes du Musée du Caire,* ed. C.C. Edgar. Cairo.

*I, (Cat. Vol. 79), 1925. Nos. 59001-59139. [MF 1.46; rp. GO]

*II, (Cat. Vol. 82), 1926. Nos. 59140-59297. [MF 1.47; rp. GO]

*III, (Cat. Vol. 85), 1928. Nos. 59298-59531. [MF 1.48; rp. GO]

*IV, (Cat. Vol. 90), 1931. Nos 59532-59800. [MF 1.49; rp. GO]

*V, ed. from Edgar's notes posthumously by O. Guéraud and P. Jouguet. 1940. Nos. 59801-59853. (Publ.Soc.Fouad V). [MF 1.50; rp. GO]

*P.Charite = *Das Aurelia Charite Archiv,* ed. K.A. Worp. Zutphen 1980. (Stud.Amst. XII). Nos. 1-41. [o.e. TPC] An additional Charite text appears in *CPR* XVIIA, pp.78-79.

P.Chic. = *Chicago Literary Papyri,* ed. E.J. Goodspeed. Chicago 1908. Nos. 1-7. [MF 2.107] See also *P.Kar.Goodsp.*

(*)P.Col. = *Columbia Papyri.*

*I, *Upon Slavery in Ptolemaic Egypt* (P.Col.inv. 480), by W.L. Westermann. New York 1929. [Rp. CG]

*II, *Tax Lists and Transportation Receipts from Theadelphia,* ed. W.L. Westermann and C.W. Keyes. New York 1932. No. 1 recto. [Rp. CG]

*III, *Zenon Papyri: Business Papers of the Third Century B.C. dealing with Palestine and Egypt,* vol. I, ed. W.L. Westermann and E.S. Hasenoehrl. New York 1934. Nos. 2-59. [Rp. CG]

*IV (*P.Col.Zen.* II), ed. W.L. Westermann, C.W. Keyes, and H. Liebesny. New York 1940. Nos. 60-122. [Rp. CG]

*V, *Tax Documents from Theadelphia,* ed. J. Day and C.W. Keyes. New York 1956. No. 1 verso. [o.e. WHA; rp. CG]

(*)VI, *Apokrimata; Decisions of Septimius Severus on Legal Matters,* ed. W.L. Westermann and A.A. Schiller. New York 1954. No.

123. Not actually part of *Columbia Papyri*, Greek Series, but later treated as Vol. VI. Improved text ed. H.C. Youtie and A.A. Schiller in *Cd'E* 30 (1955) 327-345, repr. as *SB* VI 9526. [Rp. CG]

*VII, *Fourth Century Documents from Karanis*, ed. R.S. Bagnall and N. Lewis. Missoula 1979. (Am.Stud.Pap. XX). Nos. 124-191. [o.e. SP]

*VIII, *Columbia Papyri VIII*, ed. R.S. Bagnall, T.T. Renner and K.A. Worp. Atlanta 1990. (Am.Stud.Pap. XXVIII). Nos. 192-246. [o.e. SP]

*P.Coll.Youtie = *Collectanea Papyrologica: Texts Published in Honor of H.C. Youtie*, ed. A.E. Hanson. Bonn 1976. (Pap.Texte Abh. XIX-XX). I, nos. 1-65; II, nos. 66-121; no. 96 wooden tablet, nos. 97-120 mummy labels, nos. 121-126 ostraca. [o.e. RH]

*P.Congr.XV = *Actes du XVe Congrès International de Papyrologie* (ed. J. Bingen and G. Nachtergael) II, *Papyrus inédits*. Brussels 1979. (Pap.Brux. XVII). Nos. 1-22 Greek, no. 23 Coptic. [o.e. FERE]

*P.Corn. = *Greek Papyri in the Library of Cornell University*, ed. W.L. Westermann and C.J. Kraemer, Jr. New York 1926. Nos. 1-55. [Rp. CG]

*P.Customs = *Customs Duties in Graeco-Roman Egypt*, by P.J. Sijpesteijn. Zutphen 1987. (Stud.Amst. XVII). Within a monographic study of customs, 109 new texts and 19 republished texts are catalogued in List I (pp.102-143) among a chronological list of 919 customs transactions; the numbers denote not individual papyri but separate transactions attested, as many as 152 assigned to a single papyrus text (e.g. 733-884). The new and republished texts are edited in "Notes to List I" (pp.144-189) and fully indexed (pp.217-229). Republished are *P.Stras.* II 123, *SB* XII 10789, *Stud.Pal.* XXII 63.2-7,9-12,14 and 64.3-4,6-8,10. Five additional texts (formerly *P.Lond.* descripta) are edited in "Addenda et Corrigenda" pp.1-6, to be renumbered as 428a-d and 596a. There are plates of new texts. [o.e. TPC]

*P.David = *Antidoron Martino David oblatum, Miscellanea Papyrologica*, ed. E. Boswinkel, B.A. van Groningen, P.W. Pestman. Leiden 1968. (Pap.Lugd.Bat. XVII). Nos. 12 and 15 Demotic; 1, 3, 4, 7, 10, 14, 16 and 17 Greek papyrus documents, 5 and 18 literary; 6 two ostraca. Greek documents reprinted *SB* X 10281-10287. [o.e. EJB]

*P.Diog. = *Les Archives de Marcus Lucretius Diogenes et textes apparentés*, ed. P. Schubert. Bonn 1990. (Pap.Texte Abh. XXXIX). Nos. 1-68; nos. 1, 10-11 are Latin, the remainder Greek. [o.e. RH]

*P.Dion. = *Les archives privées de Dionysios, fils de Kephalas*, ed. E. Boswinkel and P.W. Pestman. Leiden 1982; with a separate fascicle of plates. (Pap.Lugd.Bat. XXII). Nos. 1-8 Demotic, nos. 9-41 and appendix A-B Greek. [o.e. EJB]

*P.Dura = *The Excavations at Dura Europos conducted by Yale University and the French Academy of Inscriptions and Letters, Final Report V, Part I, The Parchments and Papyri*, ed. C.B. Welles, R.O. Fink, and J.F Gilliam. New Haven 1959. Nos. 1-155 (no. 1-11 are literary or subliterary; nos. 3, 10-24, 28, 33, 35-38, 47-50, 109-112, 119, 149, 152-154 are parchment; no. 53 is a waxed tablet and no. 131 is leather). Greek, nos. 1-10, 12-25, 29, 31-53, 123, 126-127, 129, 132, 137, 140-141, 144, 146-150; Latin, nos. 54, 56-65, 67-122, 124-125, 130-131, 133-136, 138, 142-143, 145; Greek and Latin, nos. 26, 30, 55, 66, 128, 139; Greek and Aramaic, no. 27; Greek and Syriac, no. 28; Hebrew, no. 11; Aramaic, nos. 151, 152; Parthian, no. 153; Persian, nos. 154, 155. [MF 1.62]

(*)P.Edfou = papyri published in *Fouilles Franco-Polonaises* I-III, a series issued by the Institut Français d'Archéologie Orientale du Caire and the University of Warsaw. [MF 1.63]

*I, *Tell Edfou 1937*, by B. Bruyère, J. Manteuffel, K. Michalowski, J. Sainte Fare Garnot. Cairo 1937. Chap. V, pp.141-191, includes papyri I-IV; for ostraca nos. 1-230 see *O.Edfou* I.

*II, *Tell Edfou 1938*, by K. Michalowski, J. de Linage, J. Manteuffel, J. Sainte Fare Garnot. Cairo 1938. Chap. III, pp.138-166, includes papyri V-VII; for ostraca nos. 231-325 see *O.Edfou* II.

*III, *Tell Edfou 1939*, by K. Michalowski, Ch. Desroches, J. de Linage, J. Manteuffel, M. Zejmo-Zejmis. Cairo 1950. Chap. V, pp.331-372, includes papyrus VIII; for ostraca nos. 326-483 see *O.Edfou* III.

(*)Papyrus IX ed. R. Rémondon, "Soldats de Byzance d'après un papyrus trouvé à Edfou," in *RechPap* 1 (1961) 41-93. Text reprinted *SB* VI 9613.

(*)P.Edg. = "Selected Papyri from the Archives of Zenon," ed. C.C. Edgar, in *Annales du Service des Antiquités de l'Égypte*. Cairo. [MF 2.29]

Nos. 1-10, *Ann.* 18 (1918) 159-182.
Nos. 11-21, *Ann.* 18 (1918) 225-244.
Nos. 22-36, *Ann.* 19 (1919) 13-36.
Nos. 37-48, *Ann.* 19 (1920) 81-104.
Nos. 49-54, *Ann.* 20 (1920) 19-40.
Nos. 55-64, *Ann.* 20 (1920) 181-206.
Nos. 65-66, *Ann.* 21 (1921) 89-109.
Nos. 67-72, *Ann.* 22 (1922) 209-231.
Nos. 73-76, *Ann.* 23 (1923) 73-98.
Nos. 77-88, *Ann.* 23 (1923) 187-209.
Nos. 89-111, *Ann.* 24 (1924) 17-52.
Texts reprinted as *SB* III 6707-6794, 6804-6820, 6989-6994 and in
   **P.Cair.Zen.*

P.Egerton = *Fragments of an Unknown Gospel and Other Early Christian Papyri*, ed. H.I. Bell and T.C. Skeat. London 1935.

P.Egger = a papyrus published by Egger in *Bulletin de la Société des antiquaires de France*, Paris 1862, pp.123ff. See *SB* II p.58 which indicates republication in *UPZ*; it does not, however, appear there.

*P.Eleph. = *Aegyptische Urkunden aus den königlichen Museen in Berlin*: *Griechische Urkunden*, Sonderheft. *Elephantine-Papyri*, ed. O. Rubensohn. Berlin 1907. Nos. 1-32 and 3 fragments. [MF 2.81; rp. CG]

*P.Enteux. = ΕΝΤΕΥΞΕΙΣ: *Requêtes et plaintes addressées au Roi d'Égypte au IIIe siècle avant J. C.*, ed. O. Guéraud. Cairo 1931. (Publ.Soc. Fouad I). Nos. 1-113 and appendix of 4 texts. [MF 1.52]

(*)P.Erasm. *I = *Papyri in the Collection of the Erasmus University (Rotterdam)*, ed. P.J. Sijpesteijn and Ph.A. Verdult. Brussels 1986. (Pap.Brux. XXI). Nos. 1-22. [o.e. FERE]

*II = *P.Erasmianae II, Parts of the Archive of an Arsinoite Sitologus from the Middle of the Second Century B.C.*, ed. P.A. Verdult. Amsterdam 1991. (Stud.Amst. XXXII). Nos. 23-58. [o.e. JCG]. Rev. and transl. ed. of *P.Erasmianae II, Delen van een arsinoitisch sitologen-archief uit het midden van de tweede eeuw v. Chr.*, ed. P.A. Verdult. Rotterdam 1988. (Mededelingen van het Juridisch Instituut van de Erasmus Universiteit Rotterdam, nr. 45). Nos. 23-58, and one unnumbered text *P.Abcoude* (51a, pp.241-242) also reprinted as *SB* XIV 11962.

*P.Erl. = *Die Papyri der Universitätsbibliothek Erlangen*, ed. W. Schubart. Leipzig 1942. (Katalog der Handschriften der Universitätsbibliothek Erlangen, Neubearbeitung, Band III, Teil I). Nos. 1-149. [o.p.]

*P.Fam.Tebt. = *A Family Archive from Tebtunis*, ed. B.A. van Groningen. Leiden 1950. (Pap.Lugd.Bat. VI). Nos. 1-55. [MF 2.60]

P.Fay. = *Fayûm Towns and their Papyri*, ed. B.P. Grenfell, A.S. Hunt and D.G. Hogarth. London 1900. (Egypt Exploration Society, Graeco-Roman Memoirs 3). Nos. 1-366 papyri; ostraca (numbered separately) 1-50. [o.e. EES]

P.Flor. = *Papiri greco-egizii, Papiri Fiorentini* (Supplementi Filologico-Storici ai Monumenti Antichi). Milan. [Rp. BdE]

　I, *Documenti pubblici e privati dell'età romana e bizantina*, ed. G. Vitelli. 1906. Nos. 1-105.

*II, *Papiri letterari ed epistolari*, ed. D. Comparetti. 1908-1911. Nos. 106-278.

*III, *Documenti e testi letterarii dell'età romana e bizantina*, ed. G. Vitelli. 1915. Nos. 279-391.

P.Forshall = *Description of the Greek Papyri in the British Museum*, by J. Forshall. London 1839. Nos. 1-44. Mostly reprinted in *P.Lond.* I (see *SB* II pp.84-85) and *UPZ*.

*P.Fouad = *Les Papyrus Fouad I*, ed. A. Bataille, O. Guéraud, P. Jouguet, N. Lewis, H. Marrou, J. Scherer and W.G. Waddell. Cairo 1939. (Publ.Soc. Fouad III). Nos. 1-89; 45 is Latin. [MF 2.91]

*P.Frankf. = *Griechische Papyri aus dem Besitz des Rechts-wissenschaftlichen Seminars der Universität Frankfurt*, ed. H. Lewald. Heidelberg 1920. (*SBHeidelberg* 1920, Abh. 14). Nos. 1-7. An additional text at *SB* XIV 12093. [MF 1.25]

(*)P.Freer = *Greek and Coptic Papyri in the Freer Gallery of Art*, ed. L.S.B. MacCoull. Diss. Washington D.C. 1973. Microfilm order no. 73-19,867. Nos. 1-6 Greek, nos. 7-10 Coptic. *Nos. 1-2 are reedited by J. Gascou and L. MacCoull in "Le cadastre d'Aphroditô," *Travaux et Mémoires* 10 (1987) pp.103-158 with 10 plates. *Nos. 3-4 are reedited by J. Gascou in *Hommes et richesses dans l'Empire byzantin. Réalités byzantines, I: IVe-VIIe siècle* (Paris 1989) 279-313.

(*)P.Freib. = *Mitteilungen aus der Freiburger Papyrussammlung.*
  *I, *Literarische Stücke,* ed. W. Aly. *Ptolemäische Kleruchenurkunde,*
    ed. M. Gelzer. Heidelberg 1914. (*SBHeidelberg* 1914, Abh. 2).
    Nos. 1-7; no. 7 reprinted as *SB* I 5942. [MF 1.80; rp. CG]
  *II, *Juristische Texte der römischen Zeit,* ed. J. Partsch. Heidelberg
    1916. (*SBHeidelberg* 1916, Abh.10). Nos. 8-11. Texts reprinted as
    SB III 6291-6294. [MF 1.81; rp. CG]
  *III, *Juristische Urkunden der Ptolemäerzeit,* ed. J. Partsch.
    Heidelberg 1927. (*AbhHeidelberg* 1927, Abh. 7). Nos. 12-38. [MF
    1.82; rp. CG]
  (*)Nos. 39-44 are listed in *P.Freib.* IV as follows: 39 = *SB* V 7600;
    40-41 = *SB* III 6094-6095; 42 = *SB* IV 7351; 43 = *SB* VI 9562;
    44 = *P.Customs* 266.
  *IV, *Griechische und demotische Papyri der Universitätsbibliothek
    Freiburg,* ed. R.W. Daniel, M. Gronewald, H.J. Thissen. Bonn
    1986. (Pap.Texte Abh. XXXVIII). Nos. 45-71 Greek; nos. 72-75
    Demotic. [o.e. RH]
*P.Fuad I Univ. (or P.Fuad Crawford) = *Fuad I University Papyri,* ed.
    D.S. Crawford. Alexandria 1949. (Publ.Soc.Fuad VIII). Nos. 1-
    43. [MF 2.95] Cf. on the collection *P.Grad.*
P.Gen. = *Les Papyrus de Genève.*
  I, ed. J. Nicole. Geneva 1896-1906. Nos. 1-81. [MF 2.47; rp. AMH
    1967] Outside this numeration, Nicole published other papyri in
    (*)*Textes grecs inédits de la collection papyrologique de Genève*
    (Geneva 1909), nos. I-VI; nos. IV and V are documentary; No.
    IV publishes three texts reprinted as *SB* I 15-17 (15 republished
    with additions as *BGU* XIII 2216). No. V is reprinted at *SB* I 1.
  *II, ed. Cl. Wehrli. Geneva 1986. Nos. 82-117. [o.e. Bibl.Pub.Univ.]
*P.Genova I = *Papiri dell'Università di Genova* I, ed. M. Amelotti and L.
    Zingale Migliardi (*sic*). Milan 1974. Nos. 1-50. (Univ. di Genova,
    Fondazione Nobile Agostino Poggi 10). [o.e. AG]
  *II, ed. L. Migliardi Zingale. Florence 1980. (Pap.Flor. VI). Nos. 51-
    85 papyri; nos. 86-90 ostraca. [o.e. LG]
  *III, ed. L. Migliardi Zingale. Florence 1991. (Pap.Flor. XX). Nos.
    91-130. [o.e. LG]
*P.Giss. = *Griechische Papyri im Museum des oberhessischen
    Geschichtsvereins zu Giessen,* ed. O. Eger, E. Kornemann, and
    P.M. Meyer. Leipzig-Berlin 1910-1912. Part 1, nos. 1-35; Part 2,
    nos. 36-57; Part 3, nos. 58-126. [Rp. CG]

(*)P.Giss.Univ. = *Mitteilungen aus der Papyrussammlung der Giessener Universitätsbibliothek.* Giessen.

*I, *Griechische Papyrusurkunden aus ptolemäischer und römischer Zeit*, ed. H. Kling. 1924. Nos. 1-16. (Schriften der hessischen Hochschulen, Universität Giessen 1924, 4). [MF 2.20; rp. CG]

II, *Ein Bruchstück des Origenes über Genesis I, 28*, ed. P. Glaue. 1928. No. 17. (Schriften 1928, 1). [MF 2.21; rp. CG]

*III, *Griechische Privatbriefe*, ed. H. Büttner. 1931. Nos. 18-33. (Schriften 1931, 3). [MF 2.22; rp. CG]

IV, *Literarische Stücke*, ed. H. Eberhart. 1935. Nos. 34-45. (Schriften 1935, 2). [MF 2.23; rp. CG]

V, *Alexandrinische Geronten vor Kaiser Gaius: Ein neues Bruchstück der sogenannten Alexandrinischen Märtyrer-Akten*, ed. A. von Premerstein. 1939. No. 46. (Schriften der Ludwigs Universität zu Giessen, Jg. 1936). [MF 2.24; rp. CG]

*VI, *Griechische Verwaltungsurkunden von Tebtynis aus dem Anfang des dritten Jahrhunderts n. Chr.*, ed. G. Rosenberger. 1939. Nos. 47-53. [MF 2.25; rp. CG]

Indices zu den Papyri bibliothecae universitatis Gissensis (P.bibl. univ.Giss.), by K.A. Worp. 1975. (Kurzberichte 35). [MF 2.26]

*P.Got. = *Papyrus grecs de la Bibliothèque municipale de Gothembourg*, ed. H. Frisk. Gothenburg 1929. (Göteborgs Högskolas Årsskrift 35 [1929] Part 1) Nos. 1-21; nos. 22-114 descripta. [Rp. CG]

*P.Grad. = *Griechische Papyri der Sammlung Gradenwitz*, ed. G. Plaumann. Heidelberg 1914. (*SBHeidelberg* 1914, Abh. 15). Nos. 1-19. Texts reprinted as *SB* I 5680, III 6275-6290. Further on the collection see the introduction to *P.Fuad I Univ.* and *Archiv* 17 (1962) 263. [MF 2.19; rp. CG]

P.Grenf. I = *An Alexandrian Erotic Fragment and other Greek Papyri chiefly Ptolemaic*, ed. B.P. Grenfell. Oxford 1896. Nos. 1-70. [MF 2.105; rp. CG]

II, *New Classical Fragments and other Greek and Latin Papyri*, ed. B.P. Grenfell and A.S. Hunt. Oxford 1897. Nos. 1-113. [MF 2.110; rp. CG]

*P.Gron. = *Papyri Groninganae; Griechische Papyri der Universitätsbibliothek zu Groningen nebst zwei Papyri der Universitätsbibliothek zu Amsterdam*, ed. A.G. Roos. Amsterdam 1933. (Verhandelingen der Koninklijke Akademie van Wetenschappen te Amsterdam, Afdeeling Letterkunde, Nieuwe

Reeks, Deel 32, No. 4). Nos. 1-22. The two Amsterdam papyri at the end should be cited as *P.Gron.Amst.* 1-2. No.3 has been published by P.J. Sijpesteijn, *ZPE* 11 (1973) 167-68 = *SB* XII 11229. [Rp. CG]

*P.Gur. = *Greek Papyri from Gurob*, ed. J.G. Smyly. Dublin 1921. (Royal Irish Academy, Cunningham Memoirs 12). Nos. 1-29. [MF 1.53]

*P.Hal. = *Dikaiomata: Auszüge aus alexandrinischen Gesetzen und Verordnungen in einem Papyrus des Philologischen Seminars der Universität Halle mit einem Anhang weiterer Papyri derselben Sammlung*, ed. by the Graeca Halensis. Berlin 1913. Nos. 1-22. [Rp. CG]

*P.Hamb. I = *Griechische Papyrusurkunden der Hamburger Staats- und Universitätsbibliothek* I (in 3 parts), ed. P.M. Meyer. Leipzig-Berlin 1911-1924. Part 1, nos. 1-23; Part 2, nos. 24-56; Part 3, nos. 57-117. [MF 2.103: rp. CG]

*II, *Griechische Papyri der Hamburger Staats- und Universitätsbibliothek mit einigen Stücken aus der Sammlung Hugo Ibscher*, ed. B. Snell and others. Hamburg 1954. (Veröffentlichungen aus der Hamburger Staats- und Universitäts-bibliothek 4). Nos. 118-192. [o.e. EH]

*III, *Griechische Papyri der Staats- und Universitätsbibliothek Hamburg*, ed. B. Kramer and D. Hagedorn. Bonn 1984. (Pap.Texte Abh. XXXI). Nos. 193-234. [o.e. RH]

*P.Harr. I = *The Rendel Harris Papyri of Woodbrooke College, Birmingham*, ed. J.E. Powell. Cambridge 1936. Nos. 1-165. [Rp. CG]

*II, ed. R.A. Coles, M. Manfredi, P.J. Sijpesteijn, A.S. Brown et al. Zutphen 1985. (Stud.Amst. XXVI). Nos. 166-240. [o.e. TPC]

(*)P.Haun. = *Papyri Graecae Haunienses.*

*I, *Literarische Texte und ptolemäische Urkunden*, ed. T. Larsen. Copenhagen 1942. Nos. 1-12. [Rp. CG] Documentary texts (nos. 9-12) reprinted as *SB* VI 9422-9425. Five additional texts were published in *Cahiers de l'Institut du Moyen-âge Grec et Latin* 6, Copenhagen 1971, by A. Bülow-Jacobsen and S. Ebbesen. [o.e. CIU] Reprinted as *SB* XIV 11355-11358 and 11714. *SB* XIV 11357 = *P.Haun.* III 58; 11358 = II 19.

*II, ed. A. Bülow-Jacobsen. Bonn 1981. (Pap.Texte Abh. XXIX). Nos. 13-44. [o.e. RH]

*III, ed. T. Larsen and A. Bülow-Jacobsen. Bonn 1985. (Pap.Texte Abh. XXXVI). Nos. 45-69; no.45 is Latin. [o.e. RH]

P.Haw. = Texts on pp.24-36 in *Hawara, Biahmu and Arsinoe*, by W.M. Flinders Petrie. London 1889. (Further publication of some texts by J.G. Milne, *Archiv* 5 [1913] 378-397.) There is a concordance at *SB* II, pp.126-27. [MF 2.73]

(*)P.Heid. = *Veröffentlichungen aus der Heidelberger Papyrussammlung.* See also Pap.Heid. in Section V, Series.

I (= Pap.Heid. N.F. II), *Literarische griechische Texte der Heidelberger Papyrussammlung*, ed. E. Siegmann. Heidelberg 1956. Nos. 181-209 (numbering cont. from *P.Bad.*). [o.e. CWV]

*II, Nos. 210-224, ed. J. Seyfarth in *Archiv* 16 (1958) 143-68; texts reprinted as *SB* VI 9530-9544. [o.e. CWV]

*III (= Pap.Heid. N.F. III), *Griechische Papyrusurkunden und Ostraka der Heidelberger Papyrussammlung*, ed. P. Sattler. Heidelberg 1963. Nos. 225-248 (papyri), 249-288 (ostraca). [o.e. CWV]

*IV (= Pap.Heid. N.F. V), *Griechische Texte der Heidelberger Papyrus-Sammlung*, ed. B. Kramer and D. Hagedorn. Heidelberg 1986. Nos. 289-296 literary, 297-342 documentary. [o.e. CWV]

*V (= Pap.Heid. N.F. VI), *Vertragliche Regelungen von Arbeiten im späten griechischsprachigen Ägypten, mit Editionen von Texten der Heidelberger Papyrus-Sammlung, des Istituto Papirologico "G. Vitelli", des Ägyptischen Museums zu Kairo und des British Museum, London*, ed. A. Jördens. Heidelberg 1990. Nos. 343-361. [o.e. CWV]

*P.Hels. I, *Papyri Helsingienses I, Ptolemäische Urkunden*, ed. J. Frösén, P. Hohti, J. and M. Kaimio, H. Zilliacus. Helsinki 1986. (Societas Scientiarum Fennica, Commentationes Humanarum Litterarum 80). Nos. 1-47. [o.e. AB]

P.Hercul.: See now *Catalogo dei Papiri Ercolanesi*, compiled under the direction of M. Gigante at Centro Internazionale per lo Studio dei Papiri Ercolanesi. Naples 1979, and *Manuale di papirologia ercolanese*, by M. Capasso. Lecce 1991. (Università degli Studi di Lecce, Dipartimento di Filologia Classica e Medioevale, Testi e Studi 3.)

*P.Herm. = *Papyri from Hermopolis and Other Documents of the Byzantine Period*, ed. B.R. Rees. London 1964. Nos. 1-85. (Egypt Exploration Society, Graeco-Roman Memoirs 42). [o.e. EES]

*P.Herm.Landl. = *Zwei Landlisten aus dem Hermupolites (P.Giss. 117 und P.Flor. 71)*, ed. P.J. Sijpesteijn and K.A. Worp. Zutphen 1978. Also 2 additional texts *(Stud.Pal.* V 120 and *P.Flor.* I 87 reedited) in appendices. (Stud.Amst. VII). [o.e. TPC]

P.Hib. = *The Hibeh Papyri.* London.

  I, ed. B.P. Grenfell and A.S. Hunt. 1906. Nos. 1-171. (Egypt Exploration Society, Graeco-Roman Memoirs 7). [o.e. EES]

  *II, ed. E.G. Turner and M.-Th. Lenger. 1955. Nos. 172-284. (Egypt Exploration Society, Graeco-Roman Memoirs 32). [o.e. EES]

P.Holm. = *Papyrus Graecus Holmiensis, Recepte für Silber, Steine und Purpur*, ed. O. Lagercrantz. Uppsala and Leipzig 1913. (Arbeten utgifna med understöd af Vilhelm Ekmans Universitetsfond 13). [o.e. UUB]

*P.Hombert = *La Collection Marcel Hombert* I, ed. G. Nachtergael. Brussels 1978. No. 27 papyrus; nos. 28-31 ostraca; nos. 32-34 wooden tablets; rp. *SB* XIV 11986-11991. (Pap.Brux. XV) [o.e. FERE]

(*)P.Iand. = *Papyri Iandanae*, cum discipulis ed. C. Kalbfleisch. Leipzig.

  I, *Voluminum codicumque fragmenta graeca cum amuleto christiano*, ed. E. Schaefer. 1912. Nos. 1-7. [MF 2.6]

  *II, *Epistulae privatae graecae*, ed. L. Eisner. 1913. Nos. 8-25. [MF 2.7]

  *III, *Instrumenta graeca publica et privata*, Part I, ed. L. Spohr. 1913. Nos. 26-51. [MF 2.8]

  *IV, *Instrumenta graeca publica et privata*, Part II, ed. G. Spiess. 1914. Nos. 52-68b. Nos. 68, 68a, and 68b are Latin. [MF 2.9]

  V, *Literarische Stücke und Verwandtes*, ed. J. Sprey. 1913. Nos. 69-90. [MF 2.19]

  *VI, *Griechische Privatbriefe*, ed. G. Rosenberger. 1934. Nos. 91-133. [MF 2.11]

  *VII, *Griechische Verwaltungsurkunden*, ed. D. Curschmann. 1934. Nos. 134-145. [MF 2.12]

  *VIII, *Griechische Wirtschaftsrechnungen und Verwandtes*, ed. J. Hummel. 1938. Nos. 146-155. [MF 2.13]

*P.Iand.inv. 653 = *A Sixth Century Account of Hay*, ed. T. Reekmans. Brussels 1962. (Pap.Brux. I). Text reprinted as *SB* VIII 9920. [o.e. FERE]

(*)P.IFAO = *Papyrus grecs de l'Institut Français d'Archéologie Orientale.* Cairo. (Institut Français d'Archéologie Orientale du Caire. Bibliothèque d'étude).

*I, ed. J.Schwartz. 1971. Nos. 1-40. (*Bibl.* 54). [o.e. SEVPO]

*II, ed. G. Wagner. 1971. Nos. 1-50. (*Bibl.* 55). [o.e. SEVPO]

*III, ed. J. Schwartz and G. Wagner. 1975. Nos. 1-54. (*Bibl.* 56). [o.e. SEVPO]

(*)P.Ital. = *Die nichtliterarischen lateinischen Papyri Italiens aus der Zeit 445-700*, ed J.-O. Tjäder. (Acta Instituti Romani Regni Sueciae, Series in quarto, XIX.1,2,3)

*I, Nos. 1-28. Lund 1955.

*II, Nos. 29-59. Stockholm 1982.

III, plates. Lund 1954.

*P.Jena = *Jenaer Papyrus-Urkunden*, ed. F. Zucker and F. Schneider. Jena 1926. Nos. 1-4. Texts reprinted as *SB* III 7165-7168. [MF 2.101]

P.Kar.Goodsp. = *Papyri from Karanis*, ed. E.J. Goodspeed. Chicago 1902. (Univ. of Chicago, Studies in Classical Philology III, pp.1-66). [MF 2.76] Texts reprinted in *SB* Beiheft 2, 1961. 43 texts are reprinted from *BGU*; 49 were in the possession of Goodspeed. Further publications of Goodspeed papyri are *P.Cair.Goodsp.* 28-30, *CP* 1 (1906) 167-73 (Nos. 3-12 = *SB* I 4414-4423); *CP* 3 (1908) 428-34 (*SB* I 4425). In *CP* 5 (1910) 320-22 Goodspeed published three papyri from the collection of Professor John G. Harrison. On the Goodspeed papyri in general, see *ZPE* 16 (1975) 27-32.

(*)P.Köln = *Kölner Papyri*, Opladen.

*I, ed. B. Kramer and R. Hübner. 1976. Nos. 1-57; no. 49 is Latin. (Pap.Colon. VII.1). [o.e. WDV]

*II, ed. B. Kramer and D. Hagedorn. 1978. Nos. 58-114 papyri; nos. 115-124 ostraca. (Pap.Colon. VII.2). [o.e. WDV]

*III, ed. B. Kramer, M. Erler, D. Hagedorn, R. Hübner. 1980. Nos. 125-166. (Pap.Colon. VII.3). [o.e. WDV]

*IV, ed. B. Kramer, C. Römer and D. Hagedorn. 1982. Nos. 167-202. (Pap.Colon. VII.4). [o.e. WDV]

*V, ed. M. Gronewald, K. Maresch and W. Schäfer. 1985. Nos. 203-240. (Pap.Colon. VII.5). [o.e. WDV]

*VI, ed. M. Gronewald, B. Kramer, K. Maresch, M. Parca, C. Römer. 1987. Nos. 241-281. (Pap.Colon. VII.6). [o.e. WDV]

*VII, ed. M. Gronewald and K. Maresch. 1991. Nos. 282-326. (Pap.Colon. VII.7). [o.e. WDV]

(*)P.Kroll = *Eine ptolemäische Königsurkunde*, ed. L. Koenen. Wiesbaden 1957. (Klassisch-philologische Studien 19). Text reprinted as *SB* VI 9316. New fragment of col. i (also an unplaced fragment) added in *Stud.Pap.* 21 (1982) pp.73-82, and combined col. i alone reprinted as *SB* XVI 12540; reedited as *P.Köln* VII 313.

*P.Kron. = *L'archivio di Kronion*, ed. D. Foraboschi. Milan 1971. Nos. 1-69. (Collana di testi e documenti per lo studio dell'Antichità 36). Includes many documents previously published in *P.Mil.Vogl.* [o.e. CG]

(*)P.Laur. = *Dai Papiri della Biblioteca Medicea Laurenziana*, Florence.

*I, ed. R. Pintaudi. 1976. Nos. 1-20. (Pap.Flor. I). [o.e. LG]

*II, ed. R Pintaudi. 1977. Nos. 21-50. (Pap.Flor. II). [o.e. LG]

*III, ed. R. Pintaudi. 1979. Nos. 51-125. (Pap.Flor. V). [o.e. LG]

*IV, ed. R. Pintaudi. 1983. Nos. 126-192. (Pap.Flor. XII). [o.e. LG]

V, *Papiri Laurenziani Copti*, ed. G.M. Browne. 1984. Nos. 1-13. (Pap.Flor. XIII). [o.e. LG]

*P.Leeds Mus. = *A Selective Publication and Description of the Greek Papyri in the Leeds City Museum*, ed. S. Strassi. Leeds 1983. (Proceedings of the Leeds Philosophical and Literary Society, Literary and Historical Section, XIX, 4). Nos. 1-30, descripta nos. 31-136.

P.Leid. = *Papyri Graeci Musei Antiquarii Lugduni-Batavi*, ed. C. Leemans. Leiden. (Texts mostly reedited in *UPZ*; *P.Leid.* Z reed. D. Feissel and K.A. Worp, *OMRO* 68 (1988) 97-111.)

I, 1843. Nos. A-U. [MF 2.15]

II, 1885. Nos. V-Z. [MF 2.16]

*P.Leid.Inst. = *Papyri, Ostraca, Parchments and Waxed Tablets in the Leiden Papyrological Institute*, ed. F.A.J. Hoogendijk and P. van Minnen. Leiden 1991. (Pap.Lugd.Bat. XXV). Nos. 1-10, 13-14, 19-23, 25-80 are papyri; 11-12, 24 ostraca; 15-18 waxed tablets; 81-107 descriptions of papyri. [o.e. EJB]

P.Leipz. = *Die griechischen Papyri der Leipziger Universitätsbibliothek*, ed. K. Wessely. Leipzig 1885. (Verhandlungen der königlichen Sächsischen Gesellschaft der Wissenschaften 37, pp.237-75). Nos. 1-35.

*P.Leit. = *Leitourgia Papyri*, ed. N. Lewis. Philadelphia 1963. (Transactions of the American Philosophical Society N.S. 53, pt. 9). Nos. 1-16. Texts reprinted as *SB* VIII 10192-10208. [o.e. APS]

(*)P.Lille = *Papyrus grecs* (Institut Papyrologique de l'Université de Lille).
*I, in 4 fasc., 1907, 1908, 1923 and 1928. (Vol. I appeared all together [with Fasc. 1 and 2 reprinted] in 1929 as part of the Travaux et mémoires de l'Université de Lille, hors série), ed. P. Jouguet, P. Collart, J. Lesquier, M. Xoual. Nos. 1-60. [Rp. CG]
(*)II, *Papyrus de Magdôla*, ed. J. Lesquier. 1912. Contains the papyri from Magdola in the Fayum, later reedited by Guéraud in *P.Enteux.* Nos. 1-42. [Rp. CG]
P.Lips. = *Griechische Urkunden der Papyrussammlung zu Leipzig*, ed. L. Mitteis. Leipzig 1906. Nos. 1-123; 67-80, 91-92 are ostraca. [MF 2.102; rp.CG]
P.Lond. = *Greek Papyri in the British Museum*. London. At present 7 vols. (*P.Jews* continues the numerical sequence of the London papyri, but forms a separate publication regarded as vol. VI only retroactively. Up to the end of vol. III, texts are usually cited by volume no., serial no., and page). There are separate atlases of plates to vols. I-III. [Atlases, MF 2.111, 2.112, and 2.113]
I, ed. F.G. Kenyon. 1893. Nos. 1-138. [MF 1.54; rp. CG]
II, ed. F.G. Kenyon. 1898. Nos. 139-484. [MF 1.55; rp. CG]
*III, ed. F.G. Kenyon and H.I. Bell. 1907. Nos. 485-1331. [MF 1.56; rp. CG]
*IV, *The Aphrodito Papyri*, ed. H.I. Bell, with appendix of Coptic papyri ed. W.E. Crum. 1910. Nos. 1332-1646; nos. 1494-1646 are Coptic. [MF 1.57; rp. CG]
*V, ed. H.I. Bell. 1917. Nos. 1647-1911; no. 1709 Coptic, no. 1792 Latin. [MF 1.59; rp.CG]
*VI, *Jews and Christians in Egypt; The Jewish Troubles in Alexandria and the Athanasian Controversy*, ed. H.I. Bell. 1924. Nos. 1912-1929; nos. 1920-1922 are Coptic. [MF 1.60; rp. CG, GP]
*VII, *The Zenon Archive*, ed. T.C. Skeat. 1974. Nos. 1930-2193. [o.e. BMP]
P.Lond.Lit. = *Catalogue of the Literary Papyri in the British Museum*, ed. H.J.M. Milne. London 1927. [MF 1.58; rp. CG] Contains texts of many inedita, together with descriptions of texts published previously, especially those in *Classical Texts from Papyri in the British Museum*, ed. F.G. Kenyon, London 1891.

(*)P.Lund = *Aus der Papyrussammlung der Universitätsbibliothek in Lund*, published in K. Humanistiska Vetenskapssamfundet i Lund; Årsberättelse. Years and page nos. are indicated for each part. [I-VI, MF 1.45]

I, *Literarische Fragmente*, ed. A. Wifstrand. 1934-1935, pp.53-65. Nos. 1-7.

*II, *Griechische Privatbriefe*, ed. A. Wifstrand. 1936-1937, pp.161-72. Nos. 1-5. Texts reprinted as *SB* V 8088-8092.

*III, *Kultische Texte*, ed. K. Hanell. 1937-1938, pp.119-42. Nos. 1-10. Texts reprinted as *SB* V 8741-8750 and VI 9332-9339.

*IV, *Bakchiastexte und andere Papyri*, ed. E.J. Knudtzon. 1945-1946, pp.63-78. Nos. 1-14. Texts (except no. 12) reprinted as *SB* VI 9333, 9338, 9340-9350. The texts were also published by Knudtzon with introductions, translations and commentary in his disertation, *Bakchiastexte und andere Papyri der Lunder Papyrussammlung*, Lund (Ohlsson) 1946.

V, *Zwei astronomische Texte*, ed. E.J. Knudtzon and O. Neugebauer. 1946-1947, pp.77-88.

Indices to Parts I-IV by E.J. Knudtzon. 1946-1947, pp.89-110.

*VI, *Vermischte Texte*, ed. E.J. Knudtzon. 1951-1952, pp.119-37. Nos. 1-10. Texts reprinted as *SB* VI 9351-9359.

P.Marini = *I papiri diplomatici raccolti ed illustrati*, ed. G. Marini. Rome 1805. Nos. 1-146. No. 146 is Greek, the others Latin; no. 146 republ. by R. Riedinger, *Abh.München* N.F. 85 (1979) pp.24,26; no.124 republ. as *P.Rain.Cent.* 166. Cf. *P.Ital.* I, pp.69-72.

*P.Marm. = *Il papiro vaticano greco 11*, ed. M. Norsa and G. Vitelli. Vatican City 1931. No. 1 is literary, no. 2 a document. (Biblioteca Vaticana, Studi e Testi 53). [o.e. VAT]

*P.Masada = *Masada II, The Yigael Yadin Excavations 1963-1965, Final Reports: The Latin and Greek Documents*, ed. H.M. Cotton and J. Geiger. Jerusalem 1989. Nos. 721-738 are Latin papyri, 739-747 Greek papyri, 748-749 bilingual; the ostraca (nos. 750-771 Latin, 772-794 Greek) should be cited as *O.Masada*, which see. (Israel Exploration Society, The Masada Reports). [o.e. Israel Exploration Society]

*P.Matr. = *Dieci Papiri Matritenses*, ed. S. Daris. Madrid 1990. Nos. 1-10. (Cuadernos de la Fundación Pastor de Estudios Clásicos, 36). [o.e. Ediciones Atlas, Lope de Vega 18, Apt. 840, Madrid 28014, Spain]

P.Medin.Madi, see *O.Medin.Madi*.

(*)P.Mert. = *A Descriptive Catalogue of the Greek Papyri in the Collection of Wilfred Merton.*

*I, ed. H.I. Bell and C.H. Roberts. London 1948. Nos. 1-50. [o.e. HF]

*II, ed. B.R. Rees, H.I. Bell, J.W.B. Barns. Dublin 1959. Nos. 51-100. [o.e. HF]

*III, ed. J.D. Thomas. London 1967. (Bulletin of the Institute of Classical Studies, suppl. vol. 18). Nos. 101-128. [o.e. ICS]

Nos. 129-131 ed. J.D. Thomas in *JEA* 56 (1970) 172-78; texts reprinted as *SB* XII 10886-10888.

Nos. 132-136 ed. J.D. Thomas in *JEA* 68 (1982) 283-89; nos. 132-134 repr. as *SB* XVI 12470-12472, nos. 135-136 descripta.

*P.Meyer = *Griechische Texte aus Aegypten*. I, *Papyri des Neutestamentlichen Seminars der Universität Berlin*; II, *Ostraka der Sammlung Deissmann*, ed. P.M. Meyer. Berlin 1916. Papyri nos. 1-45; for ostraca nos. 1-92, see *O.Deiss.* [Rp. CG]

(*)P.Mich. = *Michigan Papyri*. At present 16 vols. Each volume has a subtitle of its own. The numerical sequence of volumes as a single series was not established until vol. II. Vol. I is often referred to as *P.Mich.Zen.*

*I, *Zenon Papyri*, ed. C.C. Edgar. Ann Arbor 1931. (Univ. of Mich. Studies, Humanistic Series 24). Nos. 1-120. [MF 1.19]

*II, *Papyri from Tebtunis*, Part I, ed. A.E.R. Boak. Ann Arbor 1933. (Univ. of Mich. Studies, Humanistic Series 28). Nos. 121-128. (Nos. 129-130, *A Papyrus Codex of the Shepherd of Hermas*, ed. C. Bonner. Ann Arbor 1934. [Univ. of Mich. Studies, Humanistic Series 22]). [MF 1.20]

*III, *Miscellaneous Papyri*, ed. J.G. Winter and others. Ann Arbor 1936. (Univ. of Mich. Studies, Humanistic Series 40). Nos. 131-221. (No. 222, *A Third Century Codex of the Epistles of Paul*, ed. H.A. Sanders, Ann Arbor 1935. [Univ. of Mich. Studies, Humanistic Series 38]. For Nos. 167 and 168 see Vol. VII.). [MF 1.21]

*IV.1, *Tax Rolls from Karanis*, ed. H.C. Youtie. Ann Arbor. 1936. (Univ. of Mich. Studies, Humanistic Series 42). Nos. 223-225. [MF 1.22]

*IV.2, *Texts nos. 357-363 and Indexes*, ed. H.C. Youtie and O.M. Pearl. Ann Arbor 1939. (Univ. of Mich. Studies, Humanistic

Series 43). [MF 1.23]   (See also *P.Cair.Mich.* for addenda to *P.Mich.* IV 359).

*V, *Papyri from Tebtunis*, Part II, ed. E.M. Husselman, A.E.R. Boak and W.F. Edgerton. Ann Arbor 1944. (Univ. of Mich. Studies, Humanistic Series 29). Nos. 226-356. [MF 1.24]

*VI, *Papyri and Ostraca from Karanis*, ed. H.C. Youtie and O.M. Pearl. Ann Arbor 1944. (Univ. of Mich. Studies, Humanistic Series 47). Nos. 364-428; ostraca nos. 700-971 (for nos. 1-699 see *O.Mich.*). [MF 1.26]

*VII, *Latin Papyri*, ed. H.A. Sanders with contributions by J.E. Dunlap. Ann Arbor 1947. (Univ. of Mich. Studies, Humanistic Series 48). Nos. 167-168, 429-463. [MF 2.17]

*VIII, *Papyri and Ostraca from Karanis*, Second Series, ed. H.C. Youtie, and J.G. Winter. Ann Arbor 1951. (Univ. of Mich. Studies, Humanistic Series 50). Nos. 464-521; ostraca nos. 972-1111 (see *O.Mich.*). [MF 2.18]

*IX, *Papyri from Karanis*, Third Series, ed. E.M. Husselman. Cleveland 1971. (American Philological Association Monograph 29). Nos. 522-576. [o.e. SP]

*X, *Documentary Papyri from the Michigan Collection*, ed. G.M. Browne. Toronto 1970. (Am.Stud.Pap. VI). Nos. 577-602. [o.e. SP]

*XI, *Papyri from the Michigan Collection*, ed. J.C. Shelton. Toronto 1971. (Am.Stud.Pap. IX). Nos. 603-625. [o.e. SP]

*XII, *Michigan Papyri XII*, ed. G.M. Browne. Toronto 1975. (Am.Stud.Pap. XIV). Nos. 626-658. [o.e. SP]

*XIII, *The Aphrodite Papyri in the University of Michigan Papyrus Collection*, ed. P.J. Sijpesteijn. Zutphen 1977. (Stud.Amst. X). Nos. 659-674. [o.e. TPC]

*XIV, *Michigan Papyri XIV*, ed. V.P. McCarren. Chico 1980. (Am.Stud. Pap. XXII). Nos. 675-684. [o.e. SP]

*XV, *Michigan Papyri XV*, ed. P.J. Sijpesteijn. Zutphen 1982. (Stud.Amst. XIX). Nos. 685-756. [o.e. TPC]

XVI, *Michigan Papyri XVI, A Greek Love Charm from Egypt (P.Mich. 757)*, ed. and comm. D.G. Martinez. Atlanta 1991. (Am.Stud.Pap. XXX). [o.e. SP]

*P.Mich.Mchl = *A Critical Edition of Select Michigan Papyri*, ed. E.M. Michael. Diss. Ann Arbor, Mich. 1966. Microfilm order no. 67-1777. Nos. 1-28. Reprinted *SB* XII 11103-11130.

*P.Michael. = *Papyri Michaelidae, being a Catalogue of Greek and Latin Papyri, Tablets and Ostraca in the Library of Mr G.A. Michaïlidis of Cairo*, ed. D.S. Crawford. Aberdeen 1955. Nos. 1-60 papyri, 61-62 wooden tablets, 63-129 ostraca. [o.e. AUP]

(*)P.Mil. = *Papiri Milanesi*, vol. I, fasc. 1, ed. A. Calderini. Milan 1928.
   *2nd ed. S. Daris, 1967. Second ed. is Vol. I of Pubblicazioni dell'Università Cattolica del Sacro Cuore, Contributi, Serie Terza, Pubblicazioni di "Aegyptus," I. Nos. 1-12. [o.e. VP]
   *II, ed. S. Daris. Milan 1966. (Pubbl., Vol. II). Nos. 13-87. [o.e. VP]

*P.Mil.Congr.XIV = *Papyri documentari dell'Università Cattolica di Milano*, ed. by various editors. Milan 1974. 43 unnumbered documents. (*Aegyptus* 54 [1974] 1-140 with Plates I-XXX). Reprinted in *SB* XIV 11264-11305.

*P.Mil.Congr.XVII = *Papiri documentari dell'Università Cattolica di Milano*, ed. O. Montevecchi et al. Milan 1983. 17 unnumbered documents. (*Aegyptus* 63 [1983] 1-102). Reprinted in *SB* XVI 12720-12740.

*P.Mil.Congr.XVIII = *Papiri documentari dell'Università Cattolica di Milano*, ed. by various editors. Milan 1986. 15 unnumbered documents. (*Aegyptus* 66 [1986] 1-70 with Plates 1-14).

*P.Mil.Congr. XIX = *Papiri documentari dell'Università Cattolica di Milano*, ed. by various editors. Milan 1989. 12 unnumbered documents. (*Aegyptus* 69 [1989] 5-60).

(*)P.Mil.Vogl.
   *I, *Papiri della R. Università di Milano*, ed. A. Vogliano. Milan 1937. Sometimes called *P.Mil.R.Univ.*, *PRIMI* or *P.R.U.M.*, to distinguish this from the series of *P.Mil.* Reprint Milan 1966 with same title as Vols. II-IV. Nos. 1-28. Texts of nos. 23-28 reprinted in *SB* Beiheft 2, 1961. [o.e. CG]
   *II, *Papiri della Università degli Studi di Milano*, ed. by many collaborators. Milan 1961. Nos. 29-110. [o.e. CG]
   *III, Milan 1965. Nos. 111-203, plus 7 Demotic texts. [o.e. CG]
   *IV, Milan 1967. Nos. 204-257, plus 3 Coptic texts. [o.e. CG]
   V, Milan 1974. A Coptic codex edited by T. Orlandi. [o.e. CG]
   *VI, Milan 1977. Nos. 258-300. [o.e. CG]
   *VII, *La contabilità di un'azienda agricola nel II sec. d.C.*, ed. D. Foraboschi. Milan 1981. Nos. 301-308. [o.e. CG]

(*)P.Monac. = *Byzantinische Papyri in der Königlichen Hof- und Staatsbibliothek zu München*, ed. A. Heisenberg and L. Wenger.

Leipzig-Berlin 1914. Nos. 1-18. (Veröffentlichungen aus der
Papyrussammlung der K. Hof- und Staatsbibliothek zu München
I). [MF 1.42; atlas, MF 2.80] Rev. and reprinted as *P.Münch*. I,
below.

(*)P.Münch. = *Die Papyri der Bayerischen Staatsbibliothek München*.

*I, *Byzantinische Papyri der Bayerischen Staatsbibliothek München*, ed.
A. Heisenberg and L. Wenger, 2nd enl. ed. D. Hagedorn.
Stuttgart 1986. Nos. 1-18. [o.e. BTS]

II, *Papiri letterari greci*, ed. A. Carlini. Stuttgart 1986. Nos. 19-44. [o.e.
BTS]

*III pt. 1, *Griechische Urkundenpapyri der Bayerischen
Staatsbibliothek München*, ed. U. and D. Hagedorn, R. Hübner,
J.C. Shelton. Stuttgart 1986. Nos. 45-154. [o.e. BTS]

(*)P.Mur. = *Discoveries in the Judaean Desert of Jordan*. Oxford. I, 1955;
IV, 1965, V, 1968, and VI, 1977, contain no Greek texts.

*II (with separate volume of plates), *Les grottes de Murabba'ât*, ed. P.
Benoit, J.T. Milik, R. de Vaux. 1961. Nos. 89-157 are Greek,
158-159 Latin. Texts nos. 89-91, 94, 114-117 reprinted as *SB* X
10300-10307. [o.e. OUP]

III, *Les petites grottes de Qumrân*, ed. M. Baillet, J.T. Milik, R. de
Vaux. 1962. 2 Greek texts, *Exodus, Letter of Jeremiah*, from 7Q,
and Greek fragments. [o.e. OUP]

*P.Nag Hamm. = *Nag Hammadi Codices. Greek and Coptic Papyri from
the Cartonnage of the Covers*, ed. J.W.B. Barns, G.M. Browne,
J.C. Shelton. Leiden 1981. (Nag Hammadi Studies XVI). Nos. 1-
153 (Greek), C1-C19 (Coptic). [o.e. EJB]

*P.Neph. = *Das Archiv des Nepheros und verwandte Texte*. Part I, *Das
Archiv des Nepheros*, ed. B. Kramer, J.C. Shelton, G.M. Browne.
Nos. 1-14, 17-42 Greek, nos. 15-16 Coptic. Part II, *Verwandte
Texte aus der Heidelberger Papyrussammlung*, ed. B. Kramer. Nos.
43-49. Mainz 1987. (Aegypt. Trev. IV). [o.e. PvZ]

(*)P.Ness. = *Excavations at Nessana*.

I, Introductory volume (pp.259-62 contain a summary by P.
Mayerson of Nessana papyri relating to agriculture), ed. H.D.
Colt. London 1962.

II, *Literary Papyri*, ed. L. Casson and E.L. Hettich. Princeton 1950.
Nos 1-13. [o.e. PUP]

*III, *Non-Literary Papyri*, ed. C.J. Kraemer, Jr. Princeton 1958. Nos.
14-195. [o.e. PUP]

(*)P.NYU = *Greek Papyri in the Collection of New York University.*
 *I, *Fourth Century Documents from Karanis*, ed. N. Lewis. Leiden
 1967. (New York Univ., Department of Classics, Monographs on
 Mediterranean Antiquity I). Nos. 1-25. [o.e. NYU or EJB]

(*)P.Oslo = *Papyri Osloenses.* Oslo.
 I, *Magical Papyri*, ed. S. Eitrem. 1925. Nos. 1-6. [o.p.]
 *II, ed. S. Eitrem and L. Amundsen. 1931. Nos. 7-64. [o.p.]
 *III, ed. S. Eitrem and L. Amundsen. 1936. Nos. 65-200. [o.e. UF]

*P.Oxf. = *Some Oxford Papyri*, ed. E.P. Wegener. Leiden 1942 (text),
 1948 (plates). (Pap.Lugd.Bat. IIIA and IIIB). Nos. 1-19. [MF
 2.57]

(*)P.Oxy. = *The Oxyrhynchus Papyri.* Published by the Egypt Exploration
 Society in Graeco-Roman Memoirs. London. The number in
 parentheses at the end of each entry is the number in this series.
 Earlier vols. carry the heading of Egypt Exploration Fund,
 Graeco-Roman Branch; even after the title change numbers
 were not assigned to the volumes until the 1950s. The system
 followed here is that adopted retroactively by the EES. [all vols.
 o.e. EES]

*I, Nos. 1-207, ed. B.P. Grenfell and A.S. Hunt. 1898. (1)
*II, Nos. 208-400, ed. B.P. Grenfell and A.S. Hunt. 1899. (2).
*III, Nos. 401-653, ed. B.P. Grenfell and A.S. Hunt. 1903. (5)
*IV, Nos. 654-839, ed. B.P. Grenfell and A.S. Hunt. 1904. (6)
V, Nos. 840-844, ed. B.P. Grenfell and A.S. Hunt. 1908. (8)
*VI, Nos. 845-1006, ed. B.P. Grenfell and A.S. Hunt. 1908. (9)
*VII, Nos. 1007-1072, ed. A.S. Hunt. 1910. (10)
*VIII, Nos. 1073-1165, ed. A.S. Hunt. 1911. (11)
*IX, Nos. 1166-1223, ed. A.S. Hunt. 1912. (12)
*X, Nos. 1224-1350, ed. B.P. Grenfell and A.S. Hunt. 1914. (13)
XI, Nos. 1351-1404, ed. B.P. Grenfell and A.S. Hunt. 1915. (14)
*XII, Nos. 1405-1593, ed. B.P. Grenfell and A.S. Hunt. 1916. (15)
XIII, Nos. 1594-1625, ed. B.P. Grenfell and A.S. Hunt. 1919. (16)
*XIV, Nos. 1626-1777, ed. B.P. Grenfell and A.S. Hunt. 1920. (17)
XV, Nos. 1778-1828, ed. B.P. Grenfell and A.S. Hunt. 1922. (18)
*XVI, Nos. 1829-2063, ed. B.P. Grenfell, A.S. Hunt, and H.I. Bell.
 1924. (19)
No.2064 was published in *Two Theocritus Papyri*, ed. A.S. Hunt and
 J. Johnson. London 1930. (22)
*XVII, Nos. 2065-2156, ed. A.S. Hunt. 1927. (20)

*XVIII, Nos. 2157-2207, ed. E. Lobel, C.H. Roberts, E.P. Wegener. 1941. (26)

*XIX, Nos. 2208-2244, ed. E. Lobel, E.P. Wegener, C.H. Roberts, H.I. Bell. 1948. (27)

*XX, Nos. 2245-2287, ed. E. Lobel, E.P. Wegener, C.H. Roberts. 1952. (29)

XXI, Nos. 2288-2308, ed. E. Lobel. 1951. (30)

*XXII, Nos. 2309-2353, ed. E. Lobel and C.H. Roberts. 1954. (31)

XXIII, Nos. 2354-2382, ed. E. Lobel. 1956. (34)

*XXIV, Nos. 2383-2425, ed. E. Lobel, C.H. Roberts, E.G. Turner, J.W.B. Barns. 1957. (35)

XXV, Nos. 2426-2437, ed. E. Lobel and E.G. Turner. 1959. (36)

XXVI, Nos. 2438-2451, ed. E. Lobel. 1961. (38)

*XXVII, Nos. 2452-2480, ed. E.G. Turner, J.R. Rea, L. Koenen, J.M.F. Pomar. 1962. (39)

XXVIII, Nos. 2481-2505, ed. E. Lobel. 1962. (40)

XXIX, No. 2506, ed. D. Page. 1963. (41)

XXX, Nos. 2507-2530, ed. E. Lobel. 1964. (44)

*XXXI, Nos 2531-2616, ed. J.W.B. Barns, P.J. Parsons, J.R. Rea, E.G. Turner. 1966. (45)

XXXII, Nos. 2617-2653, ed. E. Lobel. 1967. (46)

*XXXIII, Nos. 2654-2682, ed. P.J. Parsons, J.R. Rea, E.G. Turner. 1968. (48)

*XXXIV, Nos. 2683-2732, ed. L. Ingrams, P. Kingston, P.J. Parsons, J.R. Rea. 1968. (49)

XXXV, Nos. 2733-2744, ed. E. Lobel. 1968. (50)

*XXXVI, Nos. 2745-2800, ed. R.A. Coles, D. Foraboschi, A.H. Soliman el-Mosallamy, J.R. Rea, U. Schlag, and others. 1970. (51)

XXXVII, Nos. 2801-2823, ed. E. Lobel. 1971. (53)

*XXXVIII, Nos. 2824-2877, ed. G.M. Browne, J.D. Thomas, E.G. Turner, M.E. Weinstein and others. 1971. (54)

XXXIX, Nos. 2878-2891, ed. E. Lobel. 1972. (55)

*XL, Nos. 2892-2942, ed. J.R. Rea. 1972. (56)

*XLI, Nos. 2943-2998, ed. G.M. Browne, R.A. Coles, J.R. Rea, J.C. Shelton, E.G. Turner and others. 1972. (57)

*XLII, Nos. 2999-3087, ed. P.J. Parsons. 1974. (58)

*XLIII, Nos. 3088-3150, ed. J.R. Rea and others. 1975. (60)

*XLIV, Nos. 3151-3208, ed. A.K. Bowman, M.W. Haslam, J.C. Shelton, J.D. Thomas. 1976. (62)

*XLV, Nos. 3209-3266, ed. A.K. Bowman, M.W. Haslam, S.A. Stephens, M.L. West and others. 1977. (63)

*XLVI, Nos. 3267-3315, ed. J.R. Rea. 1978. (65)

*XLVII, Nos. 3316-3367, ed. R.A. Coles and M.W. Haslam, with contributions from 8 others. 1980. (66)

*XLVIII, Nos. 3368-3430, ed. M. Chambers, W.E.H. Cockle, J.C. Shelton and E.G. Turner. 1981. (67)

*XLIX, Nos. 3431-3521, ed. A. Bülow-Jacobsen and J.E.G. Whitehorne. 1982. (69)

*L, Nos. 3522-3600, ed. A.K. Bowman and others. 1983. (70)

*LI, Nos. 3601-3646, ed. J.R. Rea. 1984. (71)

*LII, Nos. 3647-3694, ed. H.M. Cockle. 1984. (72)

LIII, Nos. 3695-3721, ed. M.W. Haslam. 1986. (73)

*LIV, Nos. 3722-3776, ed. R.A. Coles, H. Maehler, P.J. Parsons, with contributions from others. 1987. (74)

*LV, Nos. 3777-3821, ed. J.R. Rea. 1988. (75)

*LVI, Nos. 3822-3875, ed. M.G. Sirivianou, with contributions by H.-C. Günther, P.J. Parsons, P. Schubert and others. 1989. (76)

*LVII, Nos. 3876-3914, ed. M.W. Haslam, H. El-Maghrabi, and J.D. Thomas. 1990. (77)

*LVIII, Nos. 3915-3962, ed. J.R. Rea. 1991. (78)

*P.Oxy.Hels. = *Fifty Oxyrhynchus Papyri*, ed. H. Zilliacus, J. Frösén, P. Hohti, J. Kaimio, M. Kaimio. Helsinki 1979. (Societas Scientiarum Fennica, Commentationes Humanarum Litterarum 63). Nos. 1-50. [o.e. AB]

*P.Panop. = *Urkunden aus Panopolis*, ed. L.C. Youtie, D. Hagedorn, H.C. Youtie. Bonn 1980. Nos. 1-31. [o.e. RH] Reprint of original publication in three articles (I, II, III) in *ZPE* 7 (1971) 1-40; 8 (1971) 207-34; and 10 (1973) 101-70, from which texts reprinted as *SB* XII 10968-10981, 10992-10996, 11213-11224.

*P.Panop.Beatty = *Papyri from Panopolis in the Chester Beatty Library Dublin*, ed. T.C. Skeat. Dublin 1964. Nos. 1-2. (Chester Beatty Monographs I). [o.e. HF]

P.Paris = *Notices et textes des papyrus du Musée du Louvre et de la Bibliothèque Impériale* (Notices et extraits des manuscrits de la Bibliothèque Impériale et autres bibliothèques 18.2), ed. A.J. Letronne, W. Brunet de Presle and E. Egger. Paris 1865.

Separate volume of plates. Papyri nos. 1-71, mostly republished in *UPZ*; ostraca nos. 1-13, mostly republished in *WO* II; 8 mummy labels. [MF 2.66 (incl. plates); rp. CG (text only)]

*P.Petaus = *Das Archiv des Petaus*, ed. U. Hagedorn, D. Hagedorn, L.C. Youtie and H.C. Youtie. Cologne/Opladen 1969. Nos. 1-127. (Pap.Colon. IV). [o.e. WDV]

P.Petersb. = *Catalogue des manuscrits grecs de la Bibliothèque Impériale Publique*, ed. E. de Muralt. St. Petersburg 1864. Some texts now in *P.Ross.Georg.*; cf. *SB* II p.61.

P.Petr. = *The Flinders Petrie Papyri*. Dublin. (Royal Irish Academy, Cunningham Memoirs).

   I, ed. J.P. Mahaffy. 1891. (Memoirs VIII), and pt. II, plates. Nos. 1-30. [MF 1.29; rp. CG]

   II, ed. J.P. Mahaffy. 1893. (Memoirs IX), and plates. Nos. 1-50. [MF 1.30; rp. CG]

   III, ed. J.P. Mahaffy and J.G. Smyly. 1905. (Memoirs XI), and plates. Nos. 1-146. [MF 1.31]

*P.Petr.[2] I = *The Petrie Papyri, Second Edition*. Vol. 1, *The Wills*, ed. W. Clarysse. Brussels 1991. Nos. 1-31. (Coll.Hellen. II).

*P.Phil. = *Papyrus de Philadelphie*, ed. J. Scherer. Cairo 1947. Nos. 1-35. (Publ.Soc.Fouad VII). [MF 2.94]

P.Pisa Lit. = *Papiri letterari greci*, ed. A. Carlini et al. Pisa 1978. 38 literary and subliterary fragments from Pisa and other collections; for nos. 30-38, see now *P.Münch.* II.

*P.Prag. I = *Papyri Graecae Wessely Pragenses*, ed. R. Pintaudi, R. Dostálová, L. Vidman. Firenze 1988. (Pap. Flor. XVI). Nos. 1-117. [o.e. LGF]. See also *P.Prag.Varcl* following, before 1988 cited as *P.Prag.*

(*)P.Prag.Varcl = *Papyri Wessely Pragenses*, ed. L. Varcl, in *Listy Filologické*. (Before 1988 known as *P.Prag.*) [MF 2.70]

   *I, *LF* 70 (1946) 273-86 (*SB* VI 9052-9064).

   *II, *LF* 71 (1947) 177-85 (*SB* VI 9072-9083).

   *N.S. A new series of Theadelphia papyri begins in 1957:

   Nos. 1-3, *LF* (Suppl. *Eunomia*) 80 (1957) 16-31 and 56-80 (*SB* VI 9406-9408).

   Nos. 4-8, *LF* (*Eun.*) 81 (1958) 6-27 (*SB* VI 9409).

   Nos. 9-10, *LF* (*Eun.*) 81 (1958) 69-77 (*SB* VI 9409).

   Nos. 11-17, *LF* (*Eun.*) 82 (1959) 3-18 (*SB* VI 9410).

   Nos. 18-21, *LF* (*Eun.*) 82 (1959) 81-86 (*SB* VI 9411-9414).

Nos. 22-33, *LF* (*Eun.*) 83 (1960) 16-25 (*SB* VI 9415).

Nos. 34-39, *LF* (*Eun.*) 83 (1960) 50-55 (*SB* VI 9415).

Nos. 40-53, *LF* (*Eun.*) 84 (1961) 37-46 (SB VI 9415).

(*)P.Princ. = *Papyri in the Princeton University Collections.*

　*I, ed. A.C. Johnson and H.B. van Hoesen. Baltimore 1931. (The
　Johns Hopkins Univ. Studies in Archaeology X). Nos. 1-14. [MF
　2.36; rp. CG]

　*II, ed. E.H. Kase, Jr. Princeton 1936. (Princ. Stud. Pap. I). Nos. 15-
　107. [MF 2.37; rp. CG]

　*III, ed. A.C. Johnson and S.P. Goodrich. Princeton 1942. (Princ.
　Stud. Pap. IV). Nos. 108-191. [MF 2.38; rp. CG]

(*)P.Princ.Roll = *A Papyrus Roll in the Princeton Collection*, ed. E.H.
　Kase, Jr. Baltimore 1933. [MF 2.71] Text reprinted as *SB* V
　7621. *A new edition by R.S. Bagnall and K.A. Worp in *Archiv*
　30 (1984) pp.53-82.

P.Princ.Scheide = *The John H. Scheide Biblical Papyri: Ezekiel*, ed. A.C.
　Johnson, H.S. Gehman and E.H. Kase, Jr. Princeton 1938.
　(Princ. Stud. Pap. III). [o.e. WHA]

*P.Quseir = "Papyri and Ostraka from Quseir al Qadim," ed. R.S.
　Bagnall, in *BASP* 23 (1986) pp.1-60 and plates 1-27. Nos. 1-23
　are papyri (3 Latin), 24-48 ostraca (3 Latin), 49-74 dipinti, 75
　mummy label, 76 inscription on mica.

*P.Rain.Cent. = *Festschrift zum 100-jährigen Bestehen der
　Papyrussammlung der Österreichischen Nationalbibliothek,
　Papyrus Erzherzog Rainer.* Vienna 1983. Nos. 1-166. Separate
　volume of plates. [o.e. ÖNB]

P.Rain.Unterricht = *Neue Texte aus dem antiken Unterricht*, ed. H.
　Harrauer and P.J. Sijpesteijn. Vienna 1985. (*MPER* N.S. XV).
　Nos. 1-184, school exercises, pen trials etc.; separate volume of
　plates. [o.e. ÖNB]

P.Rein. I = *Papyrus grecs et démotiques recueillis en Égypte*, ed. T.
　Reinach, W. Spiegelberg and S. de Ricci. Paris 1905. Nos. 1-58
　Greek. There are also 7 Demotic texts and one Greek literary
　ostracon. Nos. 7-40 reedited in *P.Dion. [Rp. CG]

　*II, *Les Papyrus Théodore Reinach*, ed. P. Collart. Cairo 1940.
　(*BIFAO* 39). Nos. 59-119 papyri; 120-143 ostraca. [MF 2.46]

(*)P.Rev. = *Revenue Laws of Ptolemy Philadelphus*, ed. B.P. Grenfell.
　Oxford 1896. *Reedited by J. Bingen in *SB* Beiheft 1, 1952. [MF
　1.51; Bh. MF 2.75]

(*)P.Ross.Georg. = *Papyri russischer und georgischer Sammlungen.* Tiflis. [Rp. AMH]

I, *Literarische Texte,* ed. G. Zereteli. 1925. Nos. 1-24. [MF 2.1]

*II, *Ptolemäische und frührömische Texte,* ed. O. Krüger. 1929. Nos. 1-43. [MF 2.2]

*III, *Spätrömische und byzantinische Texte,* ed. G. Zereteli and P. Jernstedt. 1930. Nos. 1-57. [MF 2.3]

*IV, *Die Kome-Aphrodito Papyri der Sammlung Lichacov,* ed. P. Jernstedt. 1927. Nos. 1-27. [MF 2.4]

*V, *Varia,* ed. G. Zereteli and P. Jernstedt. 1935. Nos. 1-73. [MF 2.5]

(*)P.Ryl. = *Catalogue of the Greek Papyri in the John Rylands Library, Manchester.* Manchester.

I, *Literary Texts,* ed. A.S. Hunt. 1911. Nos. 1-61. [o.e. JRL]

*II, *Documents of the Ptolemaic and Roman Periods,* ed. J. de M. Johnson, V. Martin and A.S. Hunt. 1915. Nos. 62-456. [o.e. JRL]

III, *Theological and Literary Texts,* ed. C.H. Roberts. 1938. Nos. 457-551. [o.e. JRL]

*IV, *Documents of the Ptolemaic, Roman and Byzantine Periods,* ed. C.H. Roberts and E.G. Turner. 1952. Nos. 552-717. [o.e. JRL]

*P.Sakaon = *The Archive of Aurelius Sakaon: Papers of an Egyptian Farmer in the last Century of Theadelphia,* ed. G.M. Parássoglou. Bonn 1978. Nos. 1-98; 78-81,83,85,88,90-91 are ostraca. (Pap.Texte Abh. XXIII). [o.e. RH]

*P.Sarap. = *Les Archives de Sarapion et de ses fils: une exploitation agricole aux environs d'Hermoupolis Magna (de 90 à 133 p.C),* ed. J. Schwartz. Cairo 1961. Nos. 1-103. (Institut Français d'Archéologie Orientale, *Bibliothèque d'Étude* 29). [o.e. SEVPO]

(*)P.Sarga = *Wadi Sarga, Coptic and Greek Texts,* ed. W.E. Crum and H.I. Bell, with an introduction by R. Campbell Thompson. Copenhagen 1922. (Coptica III). The Greek texts are listed on p. xv; no. 9 is on vellum, nos. 12, 175, 176 on papyrus, the remainder on ostraca (= *O.Sarga*).

(*)P.Schow = *Charta papyracea graece scripta Musei Borgiani Velitris qua series incolarum Ptolemaidis Arsinoiticae in aggeribus et fossis operantium exhibetur,* ed. N. Schow. Rome 1788. Text republished as *SB I 5124.

P.Schub. = *Griechische literarische Papyri,* ed. W. Schubart. Berlin 1950. (Berichte über die Verhandl. der Sächsischen Akademie der Wissenschaften Leipzig, Phil.-Hist. Kl. 97, No. 5). [Rp. CG]

*P.Select. = *Papyri Selectae*, ed. E. Boswinkel, P.W. Pestman, P.J. Sijpesteijn. Leiden 1965. Nos. 1-24 papyri; no. 25 mummy labels (i-ii) and ostraca (iii-vi). (Pap.Lugd.Bat. XIII). [o.e. EJB]

(*)PSI = *Papiri greci e latini* (Pubblicazioni della Società Italiana per la ricerca dei papiri greci e latini in Egitto). Florence. The first eleven volumes were edited by a number of persons under the general direction of G. Vitelli and M. Norsa. A list of reeditions of documentary texts is given by P. Pruneti in *Pap.Flor.* XIX.2 475-502.

*I, 1912. Nos. 1-112. [MF 1.65; rp. Bd'E]

II, 1913. Nos. 113-156. [MF 1.66; rp. Bd'E]

*III, 1914. Nos. 157-279. Nos. 254-279 are ostraca. [MF 1.67]

*IV, 1917. Nos. 280-445. [MF 1.68]

*V, 1917. Nos. 446-550. No. 460 is an ostracon. [MF 1.69]

*VI, 1920. Nos 551-730. [MF 1.70]

*VII, 1925. Nos. 731-870. [MF 1.71; rp. Bd'E]

*VIII, 1927. Nos. 871-1000. Nos. 983-1000 are ostraca. [MF 1.72]

*IX, 1929. Nos. 1001-1096. [MF 1.74; rp. Bd'E]

*X, 1932. Nos. 1097-1181. [MF 1.75; rp. Bd'E]

XI, 1935. Nos. 1182-1222. [MF 1.76; rp. Bd'E]

*XII, fasc. I, ed. M. Norsa; fasc. II, ed. V. Bartoletti. 1943-1951. Nos. 1223-1295; nos. 1268-1271 are ostraca. [MF 2.88; o.e. FL]

*XIII, ed. M. Norsa and V. Bartoletti. 1949-1953. Nos. 1296-1370. [MF 2.89; fasc. 2 only, o.e. FL]

*XIV, ed. V. Bartoletti. 1957. Nos. 1371-1452. [o.e. FL]

XV, fasc. 1, ed. V. Bartoletti and M. Manfredi. 1979. Nos. 1453-1468 (literary). [o.e. FL]

*PSI XV estr. = *Dai Papiri della Società Italiana, Estratto dal vol. XV dei P.S.I.*, ed. M. Manfredi. Florence 1966. This volume contains *PSI* XV 1478-79, 1484, 1489, 1508, 1513-14, 1522, 1526, 1532, 1536-38, 1540, 1546, 1557, 1562, 1564-66, 1569. [o.e. FL] Another *Estratto dal vol. XV*, ed. A. Biscardi, Florence 1978, has 1515. In addition: *PSI* XV 1528 = *SB* XII 11046

                          1531 = *SB* XII 11047

                          1543 = *SB* XII 11049

                          1544 = *SB* XII 11048

                          1556 = *SB* XII 11050

                          1561 = *SB* XII 11052

                          1563 = *SB* XII 11051

There are also *PSI* texts at (*)*SB* XII 11145-11155.

*PSI Congr.XI (formerly PSI Omaggio) = *Dai papiri della Società Italiana: Omaggio all'XI Congresso Internationale di Papirologia.* Florence 1965. Nos. 1-14.

*PSI Congr.XVII = *Trenta testi greci da papiri letterari e documentari editi in occasione del XVII Congresso Internazionale di Papirologia.* Florence 1983. Nos. 1-30. [o.e. IP]

*PSI Congr. XX = *Dai papiri della Società Italiana. Omaggio al XX Congresso Internazionale di Papirologia.* Florence 1992. Nos. 1-20.

*PSI Corr. I = *Correzione e Riedizioni di papiri della Società Italiana* I, ed. M. Manfredi. Florence 1977. A reedition of *PSI* 240, 835, 1148, 1150, 1156 and 1244.

PSI Od. = *Papiri dell'Odissea. Seminario papirologico 1977-78*, ed. M. Manfredi. Florence 1979. Nos. 1-14.

*P.Sorb. = *Papyrus de la Sorbonne* I, ed. H. Cadell. Paris 1966. (Publications de la Faculté des Lettres et Sciences Humaines de Paris, Série "Textes et Documents," t.X: Travaux de l'Institut de Papyrologie de Paris, fasc. IV). Nos. 1-63 are papyri, 64-68 ostraca. [o.e. PUF]

*P.Soter. = *Das Archiv von Soterichos*, ed. S. Omar. Opladen 1979. (Pap.Colon. VIII). Nos. 1-28. [o.e. WDV] Additional texts of the archive appear in *ZPE* 86 (1991) 215-29.

(*)P.Stras. = *Griechische Papyrus der kaiserlichen Universitäts- und Landesbibliothek zu Strassburg*, ed. F. Preisigke. Leipzig.

   *I, 1912. Nos. 1-80. [MF 2.39, (incl. II)]

   *II, 1920. Nos. 81-125. [See I]

   *III, *Papyrus grecs de la Bibliothèque Nationale et Universitaire de Strasbourg*, ed. P. Collomp et ses élèves. Paris 1948. (Publications de la Faculté des Lettres de l'Université de Strasbourg, fasc. 97). Nos. 126-168. [o.e. APU]

   *IV, *Papyrus grecs de la Bibliothèque Nationale et Universitaire de Strasbourg*, ed. J. Schwartz et ses élèves. Strasbourg 1963. (Publications de la Bibliothèque Nationale et Universitaire de Strasbourg I). Nos. 169-300 (with index to Nos. 126-300). [o.e. BNU]

   *V, ed. J. Schwartz et ses élèves. 1973. (*Publications* III). Nos. 301-500. [o.e. BNU]

*VI, ed. J. Schwartz et ses élèves. 1971-1975. (*Publications* IV). Nos. 501-600. Issued in fascicles 1/2, 3, 4 and 5. Nos. 501-520 were first published in the *Bulletin de la Faculté des Lettres de Strasbourg* 48 (1969-1970) 265-86. These were then re-issued with nos. 521-540 as *Publications* IV, 1/2, 1971. Index to nos. 501-800, in *Publications* X. [o.e. BNU]

*VII, ed. J. Schwartz et ses élèves. 1976-1979. Issued in fascicles 1/2, 3, 4 and 5. (*Publications* V). Nos. 601-700. Index to nos. 501-800 in *Publications* X. [o.e. BNU]

*VIII, ed. J. Schwartz et ses élèves. Nos. 701-720, *Publications* VII.1 (1980); nos. 721-740, *Publications* VII.2 (1981); nos. 741-760, *Publications* VII.3 (1982); nos. 761-780, *Publications* VII.4 (1983); nos. 781-800, *Publications* VII.5 (1984). Index to nos. 501-800 by Bärbel Kramer, *Publications* X (1986).

*IX, ed. J. Schwartz et ses élèves. Nos. 801-820, *Publications* IX.1 (1985); nos. 821-840, *Publications* IX.2 (1986); nos. 841-860, *Publications* IX.3 (1987); nos. 861-880, *Publications* IX.4 (1988); nos. 881-900, *Publications* IX.5 (1989).

(*)P.Tebt. = *The Tebtunis Papyri.*

*I, ed. B.P. Grenfell, A.S. Hunt and J.G. Smyly. London 1902. (Univ. of California Publications, Graeco-Roman Archaeology I; Egypt Exploration Society, Graeco-Roman Memoirs 4). Nos. 1-264. [o.e. EES]

*II, ed. B.P. Grenfell and A.S. Hunt. London 1907. (Univ. of California Publications, Graeco-Roman Archaeology II). Reprint 1970. (Egypt Exploration Society, Graeco-Roman Memoirs 52). Nos. 265-689 and an Appendix. The volume also includes 20 ostraca numbered separately, for which see *O.Tebt.*. [Rp. EES]

*III.1, ed. A.S. Hunt and J.G. Smyly, assisted by B.P. Grenfell, E. Lobel and M. Rostovtzeff. London 1933. (Univ. of California Publications, Graeco-Roman Archaeology III; Egypt Exploration Society, Graeco-Roman Memoirs 23). Nos. 690-825. [o.e. EES]

*III.2, ed. A.S. Hunt, J.G. Smyly and C.C. Edgar. London 1938. (Univ. of California Publications, Graeco-Roman Archaeology IV; Egypt Exploration Society, Graeco-Roman Memoirs 25). Nos. 826-1093. [o.e. EES]

*IV, ed. J.G. Keenan and J.C. Shelton. London 1976. (Egypt Exploration Society, Graeco-Roman Memoirs 64). Nos. 1094-1150. [o.e. EES]

*P.Tebt.Tait = *Papyri from Tebtunis in Egyptian and Greek*, ed. W.J. Tait. London 1977. Nos. 1-23 Demotic; 24-34 Hieratic; 35-37 Hieroglyphic; 38-53 Greek. (Egypt Exploration Society, Texts from Excavations III). [o.e. EES]

*P.Tebt.Wall = *New Texts in the Economy of Tebtunis*, ed. E.W. Wall. Diss. Duke University, Durham, N.C. 1983. Microfilm order no. 83-20613. Nos. 1-12.

(*)P.Thead. = *Papyrus de Théadelphie*, ed. P. Jouguet. Paris 1911. Nos. 1-61, all reedited in *P.Sakaon*. [Rp. CG]

*P.Theon. = *The Family of the Tiberii Iulii Theones*, ed. P.J. Sijpesteijn. Amsterdam 1976. Nos. 1-29. (Stud.Amst. V). [o.e. AMH]

*P.Thmouis = *Le Papyrus Thmouis 1, colonnes 68-160*, ed. S. Kambitsis. Paris 1985. (Université de Paris IV, Paris-Sorbonne. Publications de la Sorbonne, Série "Papyrologie" III).

(*)P.Tor. = "Papyri graeci Regii Taurinensis Musei Aegyptii," ed. A. Peyron in Reale Accademia di Torino, Classe di Scienze Morali, Storiche e Filologiche. Part 1, *Memorie* 31 (1827) 9-188, Nos. 1-2; Part 2, *Memorie* 33 (1829) 1-80, nos. 3-14. Republished in *UPZ* and *P.Tor.Amen.* except no.10. [MF 2.85]

*P.Tor.Amen. = *L'Archivio di Amenothes figlio di Horos. Testi demotici e greci relativi ad una famiglia di imbalsamatori del secondo sec. a.C.*, ed. P.W. Pestman. Milan 1981. (Catalogo del Museo Egizio di Torino, Ser. I, Monumenti e testi V). Nos. [5], 6-8 and 12 are Greek; nos. 1-4, 9-11 and 13-17 are Demotic, some with Greek subscriptions. [o.e. CG]

P.Tor.Choach. = *Il processo di Hermias e altri documenti dell'archivio dei choachiti*, ed. P.W. Pestman. Turin 1992. (Catalogo del Museo Egizio di Torino, Ser. I, Monumenti e testi VI). Nos. 1-14 in Greek and Demotic.

*P.Turner = *Papyri Greek and Egyptian edited by various hands in honour of Eric Gardner Turner on the occasion of his seventieth birthday*, ed. P.J. Parsons, J.R. Rea and others. London 1981. (EES, Graeco-Roman Memoirs, 68). Nos. 1-55. [o.e. EES]

P.Ups.8 = *Der Fluch des Christen Sabinus, Papyrus Upsaliensis 8*, ed. G. Björk. Uppsala 1938. (Arbeten utgivna med understöd av Vilhelm Ekmans Universitetsfond 47). [o.e. UUB]

*P.Ups.Frid = *Ten Uppsala Papyri*, ed. B. Frid. Bonn 1981. (Pap. Texte Abh. XXVIII) Nos. 1-10. [o.e. RH]

*P.Vars. = *Papyri Varsovienses*, ed. G. Manteuffel, L. Zawadowski and C. Rozenberg. Warsaw 1935. (Universitas Varsoviensis, Acta Facultatis Litterarum I). Nos. 1-49 papyri; 50-53 ostraca. [Rp. CG 1974 with addendum by Z. Borkowski]
Second series in "Papyri e collectione Varsoviensi. Series nova," ed. G. Manteuffel in *JJurPap* 2 (1948) 81-110. Nos. 1-8. Texts reprinted *SB* VI 9372-75.

*P.Vat.Aphrod. = *I papiri Vaticani di Aphrodito*, ed. R. Pintaudi. Rome 1980. Separate portfolio of plates. Nos. 1-26. [o.e. VAT]

*P.Vind.Bosw. = *Einige Wiener Papyri*, ed. E. Boswinkel. Leiden 1942. (Pap.Lugd.Bat. II). Nos. 1-17. [MF 2.56]

*P.Vind.Sal. = *Einige Wiener Papyri*, ed. R.P. Salomons. Amsterdam 1976. (Stud.Amst. IV). Nos. 1-23. [o.e. AMH]

*P.Vind.Sijp. = *Einige Wiener Papyri*, ed. P.J. Sijpesteijn. Leiden 1963. (Pap.Lugd.Bat. XI). Nos. 1-28. [MF 2.65]

*P.Vind.Tand. = *Fünfunddreissig Wiener Papyri*, ed. P.J. Sijpesteijn and K.A. Worp. Zutphen 1976. (Stud.Amst. VI). Nos. 1-35. [o.e. TPC]

*P.Vind.Worp = *Einige Wiener Papyri*, ed. K.A. Worp. Amsterdam 1972. (Stud.Amst. I). Nos. 1-24. [o.e. AMH]

*P.Warr. = *The Warren Papyri*, ed. M. David, B.A. van Groningen, J.C. van Oven. Leiden 1941. (Pap.Lugd.Bat. I) Nos. 1-21. [MF 2.55]

(*)P.Wash.Univ. = *Washington University Papyri*.
  *I, ed. V.B. Schuman. Missoula 1980. (Am.Stud.Pap. XVII). Nos. 1-61. [o.e. SP]
  *II, *Papyri from the Washington University Collection, St. Louis, Missouri*, Part II, ed. K. Maresch and Z.M. Packman. Nos. 62-108. Opladen 1990. (Pap.Colon. XVIII). [o.e. WDV]

(*)P.Wisc. = *The Wisconsin Papyri*, ed. P.J. Sijpesteijn.
  *I, Leiden 1967. Nos. 1-37. (Pap.Lugd.Bat. XVI). [o.e. EJB]
  *II, Zutphen 1977. Nos. 38-87. (Stud.Amst. XI). [o.e. TPC]

*P.Würzb. = *Mitteilungen aus der Würzburger Papyrussammlung*, ed. U. Wilcken. Berlin 1934. (*AbhBerlin* 1933, 6). Nos. 1-22. Rp. in U. Wilcken, *Berliner Akademieschriften zur Alten Geschichte und Papyruskunde* II, pp.43-164. Leipzig 1970. [MF 2.28]

(*)P.Yale = *Yale Papyri in the Beinecke Rare Book and Manuscript Library.*

*I, ed. J.F. Oates, A.E. Samuel and C.B. Welles. New Haven and Toronto 1967. (Am.Stud.Pap. II). Nos. 1-85. [o.e. SP]

II, ed. S.A. Stephens. Chico 1984. (Am.Stud.Pap. XXIV). Nos. 86-136. [o.e. SP]

*P.Zen.Pestm. = *Greek and Demotic Texts from the Zenon Archive,* ed. under the general direction of P.W. Pestman. Leiden 1980. (Pap.Lug.Bat. XX). Nos. 1-13 bilingual Greek and Demotic; 14-76 Greek. Appendix Nos. A-F. [o.e. EJB.]

(*)SB = *Sammelbuch griechischer Urkunden aus Aegypten* (a collection of documentary papyri, ostraca, inscriptions, mummy tablets and related texts published in journals or unindexed catalogues. Begun by F. Preisigke in 1915, continued by F. Bilabel, E. Kiessling, and H.-A. Rupprecht). In progress.

*I, Strassburg and Berlin 1913-1915. Nos. 1-6000. [MF 1.33; rp. WdG]

II, Berlin and Leipzig 1918-1922. Index to I. [MF 1.34; rp. WdG]

*III, Berlin and Leipzig 1926-1927. Nos. 6001-7269. [MF 1.35; rp. WdG]

*IV, Heidelberg 1931. Nos. 7270-7514. [MF 1.36; o.p.]

*V, Heidelberg and Wiesbaden 1934-1955. Nos. 7515-8963. [MF 1.37; o.p.]

*VI, Wiesbaden 1958-1963. Nos. 8964-9641. [o.e. OH]

VII, Wiesbaden 1964. Index to VI. [o.e. OH]

*VIII, Wiesbaden 1965-1967. Nos. 9642-10208. [o.e. OH]

IX, Wiesbaden 1969. Index to VIII. [o.e. OH]

*X, Wiesbaden 1969-1971. Nos. 10209-10763. [o.e. OH]

XI, Wiesbaden 1973. Index to X. [o.e. OH]

*XII, Wiesbaden 1976-1977. Nos. 10764-11263. [o.e. OH]

XIII, Wiesbaden 1979. Index to XII. [o.e. OH]

*XIV, Wiesbaden 1981-1983. Nos. 11264-12219. [o.e. OH]

XV, index volume not yet published.

*XVI fasc. 1 and 2, Wiesbaden 1985. Nos. 12220-12719; *fasc. 3, Wiesbaden 1988. Nos. 12720-13084. [o.e. OH]

XVII, index volume not yet published.

XVIII, Wiesbaden 1992. Nos. 13085-14068. [o.e. OH]

Beihefte, see *P.Rev.* (Bh. 1), *P.Kar.Goodsp.* and *P.Mil.Vogl.* I (Bh. 2).

(*)UPZ = *Urkunden der Ptolemäerzeit (Ältere Funde)*, ed. U. Wilcken (republication of texts published in the nineteenth century, up to but not including the Petrie papyri. There is a concordance at *BL* IV, pp.118-123.).

*I, *Papyri aus Unterägypten*. Berlin-Leipzig 1927. Nos. 1-150. [MF 2.14; rp. WdG]

*II, *Papyri aus Oberägypten*. Berlin 1935-1957. Nos. 151-229. [Rp. WdG]

II. OSTRACA AND TABLETS

*O.Amst. = *Ostraka in Amsterdam Collections*, ed. R.S. Bagnall, P.J. Sijpesteijn and K.A. Worp. Zutphen 1976. (Stud.Amst. IX). Nos. 1-108. [o.e. TPC]

*O.Ashm. = "Ostraca in the Ashmolean Museum at Oxford," in *O.Bodl.* I, pp.63-81. Nos. 1-106.

*O.Ashm.Shelt. = *Greek Ostraca in the Ashmolean Museum from Oxyrhynchus and other sites*, ed. J.C. Shelton. Nos. 1-229. Firenze 1988. (Pap. Flor. XVII). [o.e. LGF]

*O.Berl. = *Ostraka aus Brüssel und Berlin*, ed. P. Viereck. Nos. 21-99. Berlin-Leipzig 1922. (Schriften des Papyrusinstitut Heidelberg, IV). For Nos. 1-20 (Brussels ostraca), see now *O.Brux.* below. [MF 2.72]

(*)O.Bodl. = *Greek Ostraca in the Bodleian Library at Oxford and Various Other Collections.*

    *I, ed. J.G. Tait. London 1930. (Egypt Exploration Society, Graeco-Roman Memoirs 21). Nos. 1-406. This volume also contains

        O.Ashm.,

        O.Camb.,

        O.Minor and

        O.Petr., which should be cited according to those abbreviations. [o.e. EES]

    *II, *Ostraca of the Roman and Byzantine Periods*, ed. J.G. Tait and C. Préaux. London 1955. (Egypt Exploration Society, Graeco-Roman Memoirs 33). Nos. 407-2588. [o.e. EES]

    III, *Indexes*, compiled by J. Bingen and M. Wittek. London 1964. (Egypt Exploration Society, Graeco-Roman Memoirs 43). [o.e. EES]

*O.Brux. = *Au Temps où on lisait le grec en Égypte*, ed. J. Bingen. Brussels 1977. Nos. 1-20; reedition of nos. 1-20 of *O.Berl.*

*O.Buch. = *The Bucheum*, by R. Mond and O.H. Myers. 3 vols. London 1934. (Egypt Exploration Society, Memoir 41). Vols. I and III contain no Greek texts. Vol. II, The Inscriptions, ch. iii, pp.75-78, describes 26 Greek ostraca with texts of 12 ed. by A.S. Hunt, T.C. Skeat and J.G. Tait.

*O.Cair. = *Ostraka greci del Museo Egizio del Cairo*, edd. C. Gallazzi, R. Pintaudi, K.A. Worp. Florence 1986. (Pap. Flor. XIV). Nos. 1-140.

O.Cair.Cat. = *Catalogue général des antiquités égyptiennes du Musée du Caire*, nos. 9501-9711: *Griechische Ostraka*, by U. Wilcken, ed. C. Gallazzi. Cairo 1983. Not a publication of ostraca but a list and short description of ostraca in the Cairo Museum. For the texts, see *O.Cair*.

*O.Camb. = "Ostraca in the Cambridge University Library," in *O.Bodl*. I, pp. 153-73, nos. 1-141.

O.Claud. = *Mons Claudianus. Ostraca Graeca et Latina*. Cairo. (Publications de l'Institut Français d'Archéologie Orientale, Documents de Fouilles)

I, 1992, ed. J. Bingen, A. Bülow-Jacobsen, W. Cockle, H. Cuvigny, L. Rubinstein, W. van Rengen. Nos. 1-190. (Doc. XXIX). [o.e. SEVPO]

*O.Deiss. = *Ostraka der Sammlung Deissmann*, in *P.Meyer* (*Griechische Texte aus Ägypten*, ed. P.M. Meyer, II, pp.105ff. Berlin 1916) Nos. 1-92. [Rp. CG]

(*)O.Douch = *Les ostraca grecs de Douch*, ed. H. Cuvigny and G. Wagner. Cairo. (Publications de l'Institut Français d'Archéologie Orientale, Documents de Fouilles)

*I, 1986. Nos. 1-57. Documents de Fouilles XXIV/1). [o.e. SEVPO]

*II, 1988. Nos. 58-183. (Documents de Fouilles XXIV/2). [o.e. SEVPO]

*III, 1992. Nos. 184-355. (Documents de Fouilles XXIV/3). [o.e. SEVPO]

(*)O.Edfou, published in *Tell Edfou* vols. I-III; for bibliographical information see under *P.Edfou*.

*I, Nos. 1-230. Cairo 1937.

*II, Nos. 231-325. Cairo 1938.

*III, Nos. 326-372. Cairo 1950.

*O.Elkab = *Elkab III. Les ostraca grecs*, ed. J. Bingen and W. Clarysse. Brussels 1989. Nos. 1-227. [o.e. FERE]

*O.Erem. = "Griechische Ostraka in der Kaiserlichen Eremitage in St. Petersburg," ed. G. Zereteli in *Archiv* V (1913), pp.170-180, nos. 1-40.

O.Fay., see *P.Fay*.

*O.Florida = *The Florida Ostraka: Documents from the Roman Army in Upper Egypt*, ed. R.S. Bagnall. Durham, N.C. 1976. Nos. 1-31. (Greek, Roman and Byzantine Monographs 7). [o.e. GRBS]

(*)O.Heid., see *P.Heid.* N.F. III.

*O.Joach. = *Die Prinz-Joachim Ostraka*, ed. F. Preisigke and W. Spiegelberg. Strassburg 1914. (Schriften d. Wiss. Gesellschaft in Strassburg, Heft XIX). Nos. 1-22 Greek: 23-29 Demotic. Texts reprinted as *SB* III 6027-6034, 6920-6933. [Rp. CG]

*O.Leid. = *Greek Ostraka: a Catalogue of the Greek Ostraka in the National Museum of Antiquities at Leiden, with a Chapter on the Greek Ostraka in the Papyrological Institute of the University of Leiden*, ed. R.S Bagnall, P.J. Sijpesteijn, K.A. Worp. Zutphen 1980. Nos. 1-410. Descripta nos. 411-697. (Collections of the National Museum of Antiquities at Leiden IV). [o.e. TPC]

O.Lips., see *P.Lips.*

*O.Lund. = *Ostraca Lundensia. Ostraka aus der Sammlung des Instituts für Altertumskunde an der Universität zu Lund*, ed. C. Tsiparis. Lund 1979. Nos. 1-32. [o.e. from Klassiska Institutionen, Sölvegatan 2, 22362 Lund, Sweden]

*O.Masada, see *P.Masada*, Nos. 750-771 Latin ostraca, 772-794 Greek.

*O.Medin.Madi = *Ostraka e papiri greci da Medinet Madi nelle campagne 1968 e 1969*, ed. D. Foraboschi. Milan 1976. Nos. 1-33 plus two papyri (=*P.Medin.Madi*). (Collana di testi e documenti per lo studio dell'Antichità 53). [o.e. CG]

(*)O.Mich. = *Greek Ostraca in the University of Michigan Collection*,
*Part I, Texts, ed. L. Amundsen. Ann Arbor 1935. (Univ. of Mich. Studies, Humanistic Series 34). Nos. 1-699. [MF 1.27]
*II, Nos. 700-971, see *P.Mich.* VI.
*III, Nos. 972-1111, see *P.Mich.* VIII.
*IV, Nos. 1112-1144, ed. H.C. Youtie in *ZPE* 18 (1975) 267-82 (reprinted in his *Scriptiunculae Posteriores* I [Bonn 1981], no.38, pp. 237-252 [o.e. RH]) and in *SB* XIV 11499-11531.

*O.Minor = "Ostraca in Various Minor Collections," in *O.Bodl.* I, pp.174-81.

*O.Oasis = *Les Oasis d'Égypte à l'époque grecque, romaine et byzantine d'après les documents grecs*, by G. Wagner. Cairo 1987. Within a study of published and unpublished papyri, ostraca, inscriptions and graffiti referring to the Oases are edited here the following ostraca from sites listed on p.8: O.Aïn Labakha (p.82), O.Bahria nos. 2-22 (pp.88-95), O.Sarm. nos. 1-16 (pp.96-101), O.Dor. nos. 1-5 (pp.102-103), and O.Bahria div. nos. 1-16 (pp.104-109). (Institut Français d'Archéologie Orientale du Caire, Bibliothèque d'étude 100).

(*)O.Ont.Mus. (or O.ROM)
*I = Death and Taxes: Ostraka in the Royal Ontario Museum I, ed. A.E. Samuel, W.K. Hastings, A.K. Bowman, R.S. Bagnall. Toronto 1971. (Am.Stud.Pap. X). Nos. 1-72. [o.e. SP]
*II, Ostraka in the Royal Ontario Museum II, ed. R.S. Bagnall and A.E. Samuel. Toronto 1976. (Am.Stud.Pap. XV). Nos. 73-289. [o.e. SP]

*O.Oslo = Ostraca Osloënsia, Greek Ostraca in Norwegian Collections, ed. L. Amundsen. Oslo 1933. (Avhandlinger utgitt av det Norske Videnskaps-Akademi i Oslo, Hist.-Fil. Kl. 1933, No. 2). Nos. 1-28. [oe. UF]

*O.Petr. = "Ostraca in Prof. W.M. Flinders Petrie's Collection at University College, London," in O.Bodl. I, pp.82-152, nos. 1-476.

O.ROM, see O.Ont.Mus.

*O.Sarga, see P.Sarga.

*O.Stras. = Griechische und griechisch-demotische Ostraka der Universitäts- und Landesbibliothek zu Strassburg im Elsass I, ed. P. Viereck. Berlin 1923. Nos. 1-812; a few are Demotic or bilingual. [MF 1.79]

*O.Tebt., Nos. 1-20, see P.Tebt. II.

*O.Tebt.Pad. = Ostraka da Tebtynis della Università di Padova I, ed. C. Gallazzi. Milan 1979. Nos. 1-70. [o.e. CG]

*O.Theb. = Theban Ostraca, ed. A.H. Gardiner, H. Thompson, J.G. Milne. London 1913. (Univ. of Toronto Studies, Philological Series I). Texts in Hieratic, Demotic, Greek and Coptic. Nos. 1-146 are Greek. [o.e. UTP]

*O.Wilb. = Les Ostraca grecs de la collection Charles-Edwin Wilbour au Musée de Brooklyn, ed. C. Préaux. New York 1935. Nos. 1-78. [o.e. FERE; rp. CG]

O.Wilck. (or WO) = Griechische Ostraka aus Aegypten und Nubien, ed. U. Wilcken. Leipzig-Berlin 1899. 2 vols. Texts, vol. II, nos. 1-1624. Reprint Amsterdam 1970 with addenda compiled by P.J. Sijpesteijn. [MF 2.78-79; rp. CG, AMH]

There are also ostraca in the following editions of papyri: BGU VI, VII, XIV, CPR X, P.Aberd., P.Bad. IV, P.Batav., P.Coll.Youtie II,

P.Genova II, *P.Heid.* III, *P.Hombert*, *P.Köln* II, *P.Leid.Inst.*,
P.Lips., *P.Meyer*, *P.Michael.*, *P.Paris*, *P.Rein.* II, *P.Sakaon*,
P.Select, *P.Sorb.* I, *PSI* III, V, VIII, XII, and *P. Vars.* The
numbers of the ostraca are given in the citation of these volumes
in Part I. There are also ostraca throughout the volumes of *SB*.

*T.Alb. = *Tablettes Albertini, Actes privés de l'époque Vandale*, ed. C.
Courtois, L. Leschi, C. Perrat and C. Saumagne. Paris 1952.
Texts I-XXXIV; separate portfolio of plates.

*T.Varie = *Tavolette lignee e cerate da varie collezioni*, ed. R. Pintaudi,
P.J. Sijpesteijn et al. Florence 1989. (Pap.Flor. XVIII). Texts
nos. 1-81 from six collections, with 94 plates.

*T.Vindol. = *Vindolanda: the Latin Writing Tablets*, ed. A.K. Bowman
and J.D. Thomas. London 1983. (Britannia Monograph Series,
No. 4). Texts nos. 1-48, descripta 49-106, waxed tablets 107-117.

III. CORPORA

*Volumes of corpora have been entered in the Duke Data Bank of Documentary Papyri only if they contain previously unpublished texts and texts which substantial reediting has significantly improved. Such volumes are marked by an asterisk.

Chrest.Mitt. (or M.Chr.) = L. Mitteis and U. Wilcken, *Grundzüge und Chrestomathie der Papyruskunde* II. Band, *Juristischer Teil*, II. Hälfte, *Chrestomathie*. Leipzig-Berlin 1912. [MF 2.122-123 (with *Grundzüge*); rp. GO, all 4 vols.]

Chrest.Wilck. (or W.Chr.) = L. Mitteis and U. Wilcken, *Grundzüge und Chrestomathie der Papyruskunde* I. Band, *Historischer Teil*, II. Hälfte, *Chrestomathie*. Leipzig-Berlin 1912. [MF 2.120-121 (with *Grundzüge*); rp. GO, see *Chrest.Mitt.*]

Ch.L.A. = *Chartae Latinae Antiquiores*, ed. A. Bruckner and R. Marichal. Basel, Dietikon-Zürich 1954- , in progress. Vols. 1-28, 30-40 published to date. [o.e. UGV]

C.Epist.Lat. = *Corpus Epistularum Latinarum papyris tabulis ostracis servatarum*, ed. P. Cugusi. 2 vols. Florence 1992. (Pap.Flor. XXIII). Nos. 1-245. [o.e. LGF]

(*)C.Étiq.Mom. = *Corpus des étiquettes de momies grecques*, ed. B. Boyaval. Lille 1976. (Publications de l'Université de Lille III). *Nos. 1657 and 2077 were previously unedited.

C.Ord.Ptol. = *Corpus des Ordonnances des Ptolémées*, ed. M.-Th. Lenger. Brussels 1964. (Acad. Roy. de Belgique, Cl. des Lettres, *Mémoires*, coll. in 8°, vol. 57, fasc. 1). 2nd edition, corrected and updated, 1980. (*Mémoires* 64, 2). [o.e. ARB]. A further supplement appears in M.-Th. Lenger, *Corpus des Ordonnances des Ptolémées. Bilan des additions et corrections. Compléments à la bibliographie*. Brussels 1990. (Pap.Brux. XXIV). [o.e. FERE]

(*)C.Pap.Gr. = *Corpus Papyrorum Graecarum*, ed. O. Montevecchi and others.

*I, *I Contratti di baliatico*, ed. M. Manca Masciadri and O. Montevecchi. Nos. 1-40 and four appendices. Milan 1984. (Separate volume of plates.)

*II, *Il Controllo della Popolazione nell'Egitto Romano* Pt. 1, *Le Denunce di morte*, ed. L. Casarico. Nos. 1-82 and two appendices. Azzate 1985. (Separate volume of plates.)

C.Pap.Jud. = *Corpus Papyrorum Judaicarum*. Cambridge, Mass.
I, ed. V.A. Tcherikover. 1957. Nos. 1-141.
II, ed. V.A. Tcherikover and A. Fuks. 1960. Nos. 142-450.
III, ed. V.A. Tcherikover, A. Fuks and M. Stern. 1964. Nos. 451-520.

C.Pap.Lat. = *Corpus Papyrorum Latinarum*, ed. R. Cavenaile. Wiesbaden 1958. [o.e. OH]

C.Ptol.Sklav. = *Corpus der ptolemäischen Sklaventexte*, ed. R. Scholl. Stuttgart 1990. (Forschungen zur antiken Sklaverei, Beiheft 1). In three parts: I, Nos. 1-114; II, Nos. 115-260; III, Indices. [o.e. Franz Steiner Verlag]

Doc.Eser.Rom. = *Documenti per la storia dell'esercito romano in Egitto*, ed. S. Daris. Milan 1964. (Pubblicazioni dell'Università Cattolica del Sacro Cuore, Contributi, Serie Terza, Scienze Storiche IX). [o.e. VP]

Feste = *Feste pubbliche e private nei documenti greci*, ed. M. Vandoni. Milan 1964. (Testi e documenti per lo studio dell'Antichità, Serie Papyrologica VIII).

FIRA III = *Fontes Iuris Romani Antejustiniani*, pars tertia, *Negotia*, ed. V. Arangio-Ruiz. 2nd ed. Florence 1943. Reprint Florence 1969 with an appendix of material prepared by Arangio-Ruiz before his death. [o.e. GB]

Hengstl = *Griechische Papyri aus Ägypten als Zeugnisse des öffentlichen und privaten Lebens*, ed. J. Hengstl with G. Häge and H. Kühnert. Munich 1978. Republication of 161 selected documents with translation and commentary. [o.e. Heimeran]

Jur.Pap. = *Juristische Papyri*, ed. P.M. Meyer. Berlin 1920. [MF 2.45; rp. ARES]

New Docs. = *New Documents Illustrating Early Christianity*, ed. G.H.R. Horsley et al. North Ryde, N.S.W., Australia 1981- . 6 vols. to date.

Oroscopi = *Oroscopi greci. Documentazione papirologica*, ed. D. Baccani. Messina 1992. (Ric.Pap. 1). Nos. 1-18. [o.e. ES]

*Pap.Agon. = *Zehn agonistische Papyri*, ed. P. Frisch. Opladen 1986. (Pap.Colon. XIII.) Reeditions of ten papyri: 1 = *BGU* IV 1074; 2 = *BGU* IV 1073; 3 = *P.Oxy.* XXVII 2476; 4 = *P.Oxy.Hels.* 25; 5 = *P.Oxy.* XXXI 2610; 6 = *P.Lond.* III 1178; 7 = *C.P.Herm.* 121

(Stud.Pap. V); 8 = *P.Oslo* III 85; 9 = *P.Coll.Youtie* II 69; 10 = *P.Oxy.* XLIII 3116. [o.e. WDV]

*Pap.Biling. = *Recueil de textes démotiques et bilingues*, ed. P.W. Pestman with J. Quaegebeur and R.L. Vos. Leiden 1977. Part I, Transcriptions (and notes): nos. 1-3,7-10,21 Demotic; 4-6, 13-20,22,23 bilingual Greek and Demotic. No. 11 is a graffito, no. 12 a Greek inscription; nos. 15-23 are mummy labels. Part II, Traductions (and notes). Part III, Index et Planches. [o.e. EJB]

Pap.Graec.Mag. = *Papyri Graecae Magicae*, ed. K. Preisendanz. 2 vols. Leipzig-Berlin 1928, 1931. Photostatic copies of proofs of an unpublished third volume are to be found in some libraries. A reprint including texts from the projected third volume with revisions by A. Henrichs was published in 1974. [o.e. BTS] See also *The Magical Papyri in Translation*, by H.D. Betz (esp. p.xliv), Chicago 1985. See also below *Suppl.Mag.*

Pestman, *Prim.* = *The New Papyrological Primer*, being the 5th ed. of David and van Groningen's *Papyrological Primer*, by P.W. Pestman. Leiden 1990. [o.e. EJB]

Rom.Mil.Rec. = *Roman Military Records on Papyrus*, ed. R.O. Fink. Cleveland 1971. (American Philological Association Monograph 26). [o.e. SP]

Sel.Pap. = *Select Papyri* (The Loeb Classical Library). London and Cambridge, Mass.

    I, *Private Affairs*, ed. A.S. Hunt and C.C. Edgar. 1932. Nos. 1-200. [o.e. HUP]

    II, *Official Documents*, ed. A.S. Hunt and C.C. Edgar. 1934. Nos. 201-434. [o.e. HUP]

    III, *Literary Papyri: Poetry*, ed. D.L. Page. 1942. Nos. 1-147. [o.e. HUP]

Shorthand Manuals = *Greek Shorthand Manuals*, ed. H.J.M. Milne. London 1934. (Egypt Exploration Society, Graeco-Roman Memoirs 24). Includes nos. 1-6 of *P.Ant.* [o.e. EES]

Suppl.Mag. = *Supplementum Magicum*, ed. R.W. Daniel and F. Maltomini. (Pap.Colon. XVI).

    I, Opladen 1990. [o.e. WDV]

    II, Opladen 1992. [o.e. WDV]

There are also collections of letters as follows:

S. Witkowski, *Epistulae privatae graecae quae in papyris aetatis Lagidarum servantur*, Leipzig 1911 (2nd edition). Nos. 1-72.

G. Ghedini, *Lettere cristiane dai papiri greci del III e del IV secolo*, Milan 1923.

B. Olsson, *Papyrusbriefe aus der frühesten Römerzeit*, Uppsala 1925. Nos. 1-80.

W. Döllstadt, *Griechische Papyrusprivatbriefe in gebildeter Sprache aus den ersten vier Jahrhunderten nach Christus*, Diss. Jena 1934.

G. Daum, *Griechische Papyrusbriefe aus einem Jahrtausend antiker Kultur*, Paderborn 1959. Nos. 1-45.

J. O'Callaghan, *Cartas cristianas griegas del siglo V*, Barcelona 1963. (Biblioteca Histórica de la Biblioteca Balmes, ser. II 25). Nos. 1-63.

M. Naldini, *Il Cristianesimo in Egitto: Lettere private nei papiri dei secoli II-IV*, Florence 1968. (Studi e Testi di Papirologia 3). Nos. 1-97.

G. Tibiletti, *Le Lettere privati nei papiri greci del III e IV secolo d.C.*, Milan (Vita e Pensiero) 1979. (Scienze filologiche e letteratura XV). Nos. 1-34.

J.L. White, *Light from Ancient Letters*, Philadelphia (Fortress Press) 1986. Nos. 1-117.

The following are other collections of texts with varying degrees of commentary published for scholarly or pedagogical purposes:

N. Hohlwein, *L'Égypte romaine. Recueil des termes techniques relatifs aux institutions politiques et administratives de l'Égypte romaine, suivi d'un choix de textes papyrologiques*. Brussels 1912. (Acad. Roy. Belg., Mem. Cl. de Lettres, Coll. in 8°, 2 ser. VIII.) 95 selected documents with short notes are printed on pp.469-619.

A. Laudien, *Griechische Papyri aus Oxyrhynchus, für den Schulgebrauch ausgewählt*. Berlin 1912. Nos. 1-46.

R. Helbing, *Auswahl aus griechischen Papyri*. Leipzig 1924[2]. (Sammlung Göschen 625). Nos. 1-23.

G. Milligan, *Selections from the Greek Papyri*. Cambridge 1927[2]. Nos. 1-55.

W. Schubart, *Griechische Papyri. Urkunden und Briefe vom 4. Jahrh. v.Chr. bis ins 8. Jahr. n.Chr.* Bielefeld-Leipzig 1927. 1: Text; 2:

Kommentar. (Sammlung lateinischer und griechischer Schulausgaben). Nos. 1-70.

W. Hersey Davis, *Greek Papyri of the First Century.* New York-London 1933. Nos. 1-21.

H. Lietzmann, *Griechische Papyri.* Bonn 1934[4]. (Kleine Texte für Vorlesungen und Übungen 14.) Nos. 1-25.

E.J. Goodspeed and E.C. Colwell, *A Greek Papyrus Reader.* Chicago 1936[2]. Nos. 1-82.

IV. INSTRUMENTA

BL = *Berichtigungsliste der Griechischen Papyrusurkunden aus Ägypten*. I,
ed. F. Preisigke, Berlin/Leipzig 1922 [WdG]; II, ed. F. Bilabel,
in 2 parts. Heidelberg 1929, 1933; III, ed. M. David, B.A. van
Groningen, E. Kiessling. Leiden 1958 [o.e. EJB]; IV, idem,
Leiden 1964 [o.e. EJB]; V, ed. E. Boswinkel, David, van
Groningen, Kiessling. Leiden 1969 [o.e. EJB]; VI, ed. Boswinkel,
P.W. Pestman, H.-A. Rupprecht. Leiden 1976 [o.e. EJB]; VII,
ed. Boswinkel, W. Clarysse, Pestman, Rupprecht. Leiden 1986;
VIII, ed. Pestman, Rupprecht, F.A.J. Hoogendijk. Leiden 1992.
[1-4, o.p.; 5-8, o.e. EJB].

BL Bull. = *B.L. Bulletin. Liste von Neudrücken und vollständigen
Textausgaben von 1987-1992*, by N. Kruit. Leiden 1992.
(Uitgaven vanwege de Stichting "Het Leids Papyrologisch
Instituut" 13.)

BL Konkordanz = *Konkordanz und Supplement zu Band I-VII*, ed. W.
Clarysse, R.W. Daniel, F.A.J. Hoogendijk, P. van Minnen.
Leuven 1989. [o.e. Peeters]

DDBDP = Duke Data Bank of Documentary Papyri. See Preface, p.viii.
Directed by W.H. Willis and J.F. Oates, data-entry management
by L.P. Smith and C. Rine, proofing by L. Koenen and staff,
programming by D.W. Packard, W.A. Johnson and S.V.F. Waite.
Recorded by Packard Humanities Institute on PHI CD ROM 6
in April 1991, when 87 per cent complete; data entry continues.

Lexica

Calderini, *Diz.* = *Dizionario dei nomi geografici e topografici dell'Egitto
greco-romano*, ed. A. Calderini. I part 1, Cairo 1935 [rp. 1972
CG]; part 2, Instituto "Antonio de Nebrija", Madrid 1966; II, ed.
S. Daris in 4 parts. Milan 1973-1977; III, idem, in 4 parts. Milan
1978-1983; IV, idem, in 4 parts. Milan 1983-1986; V, idem,
Milan 1987. Supplemento 1 (1935-1986), ed. S. Daris. Milan
1988. [o.e. CG]

Dornseiff-Hansen = *Rückläufiges Wörterbuch der griechischen Eigennamen*, ed. F. Dornseiff and B. Hansen. Berlin 1957. (Sächsischen Akademie der Wissenschaften zu Leipzig, Phil.-hist. Kl., Berichte über die Verhandlungen 102.4). [AV] Repr. Chicago 1978 "with appendix providing a Reverse-Index of indigenous names from Asia Minor in their Greek transcriptions" by L. Zgusta. [rp. ARES]

Fachw. = *Fachwörter des öffentlichen Verwaltungsdienstes Ägyptens in den griechischen Papyrusurkunden der ptolemäisch-römischen Zeit*, by F. Preisigke. Göttingen 1915. [rp. GO]

Gradenwitz = *Heidelberger Konträrindex der griechischen Papyrusurkunden*, by O. Gradenwitz. Berlin 1931.

Kretschmer-Locker = *Rückläufiges Wörterbuch der griechischen Sprache*, ed. P. Kretschmer and E. Locker, 2nd ed. Göttingen 1963.

NB = *Namenbuch enthaltend alle griechischen, lateinischen, ägyptischen, hebräischen, arabischen und sonstigen semitischen und nichtsemitischen Menschennamen, soweit sie in griechischen Urkunden (Papyri, Ostraka, Inschriften, Mumienschildern usw) Ägyptens sich vorfinden*, ed. F. Preisigke. Heidelberg 1922. [Rp. AMH]

Onomasticon = *Onomasticon alterum papyrologicum, Supplemento al Namenbuch di F. Preisigke*, ed. D. Foraboschi in 4 pts. Milan 1967-1971. (Testi e documenti per lo studio dell'Antichità, 16). [o.e. CG]

Spoglio = *Spoglio lessicale papirologico*, ed. S. Daris, in 3 vols. Milan 1968. (Università Cattolica del Sacro Cuore, Istituto di Papirologia).

WB = *Wörterbuch der griechischen Papyrusurkunden, mit Einschluss der griechischen Inschriften, Aufschriften, Ostraka, Mumienschilder usw aus Ägypten*, ed. F. Preisigke and E. Kiessling. I A-K, 1925; II, Λ-Ω, 1927; III, besondere Wörterliste, 1931; IV parts 1-4, A-E. Berlin 1944-1971. Supplement 1 (1940-1966), ed. E. Kiessling. Amsterdam, parts 1 and 2 1969, part 3 1971. [o.e. AMH]. Supplement 2 (1967-1976), ed. H.-A. Rupprecht and A. Jördens. Wiesbaden 1991. [o.e. OH]

Grammars

Gignac, *Gram.* = *A Grammar of the Greek Papyri of the Roman and Byzantine Periods*, vol. I Phonology, vol. II Morphology, by F.T. Gignac. Milan 1976, 1981. (Testi e documenti per lo studio dell'Antichità, 55.1-2). [o.e. CG]

Mandilaras, *Verb* = *The Verb in the Greek Non-literary Papyri*, by B.G. Mandilaras. Athens 1973. [Hellenic Ministry of Culture and Sciences; available from the author, 10 Ioanninon St., Philothei, 15237 Athens, GREECE]

Mayser, *Gram.* = *Grammatik der griechischen Papyri aus der Ptolemäerzeit mit Einschluss der gleichzeitigen Ostraka und der in Ägypten verfassten Inschriften*, by E. Mayser. Berlin/Leipzig, 1923-1936. [o.e. WdG]

I, *Laut und Wortlehre*, by Mayser. 1906, rp. 1923.

I 1, *Einleitung und Lautlehre*, 2nd ed. by H. Schmoll. Berlin 1970. [o.e. WdG]

I 2, *Laut- und Wortlehre*, pt. II Flexionslehre, 2nd ed. by Mayser. 1938.

I 3, *Laut- und Wortlehre*, pt. III Stammbildung, 2nd ed. by Mayser. 1936.

II 1-2, *Satzlehre, Analytischer Teil*, by Mayser. 1933-1934.

II 3, *Satzlehre, Synthetischer Teil*, by Mayser. 1934.

Palmer, *Gram.* = *A Grammar of the Post-Ptolemaic Papyri*, by L.R. Palmer. Vol. I Accidence and Word-Formation, Part 1, The Suffixes (all published). London 1945. [OUP]

Palaeography

Boswinkel-Sijpesteijn, *Tabulae* = *Greek Papyri, Ostraca, and Mummy Labels*, by E. Boswinkel and P.J. Sijpesteijn. Amsterdam 1968. (Tabulae Palaeographicae 1). [o.p.]

Roberts, *GLH* = *Greek Literary Hands, 350 B.C. - A.D. 400*, by C.H. Roberts. Oxford 1956. [o.e. OUP]

Seider, *Pal.Gr.* = *Paläographie der griechischen Papyri*, by R. Seider. Bd. I Tafeln, Urkunden, Bd. II Tafeln, Literarische Papyri, Bd. III Text, Part 1 Urkundenschrift. Stuttgart 1967-1990. [Hiersemann]

Schubart, *Pal.* = *Griechische Palaeographie*, by W. Schubart. Munich 1925, rp. 1966. (Handbuch der Altertumswissenschaft I.4.1). [o.e. Beck]

Schubart, *PGB* = *Papyri graecae Berolinenses*, by W. Schubart. Bonn 1911. (Tabulae in Usum Scholarum, 2).

Turner, *GMAW* = *Greek Manuscripts of the Ancient World*, by E.G. Turner; 2nd ed. rev. and enl. by P.J. Parsons. London 1987. (Institute of Classical Studies, Bulletin Supplement 46). [o.e. ICS]

Handbooks

Grundz.Mitt. (or M.Gr.) = L. Mitteis and U. Wilcken, *Grundzüge und Chrestomathie der Papyruskunde*, II. Band, *Juristische Teil*, I. Hälfte, *Grundzüge*, by Mitteis. Leipzig-Berlin 1912. [MF 2.122-123 (with *Chrestomathie*); rp. GO]

Grundz.Wilck. (or W.Gr.) = L. Mitteis and U. Wilcken, *Grundzüge und Chrestomathie der Papyruskunde*, I. Band, *Historische Teil*, I. Hälfte, *Grundzüge*, by Wilcken. Leipzig-Berlin 1912. [MF 2.120-121 (with *Chrestomathie*); rp. GO]

Montevecchi, *Pap.* = *La papirologia*, by O. Montevecchi. Turin 1973. 2nd ed. Milan 1988 with additional bibliography. [o.e. VP]

Schubart, *Einf.* = *Einführung in die Papyruskunde*, by W. Schubart. Berlin 1918.

Turner, *GP* = *Greek Papyri, an Introduction*, by E.G. Turner. 2nd ed. Oxford 1980. [o.e. OUP]

V. SERIES

Aegypt.Trev. = *Aegyptiaca Treverensia.* Trierer Studien zum griechisch-römischen Ägypten. Mainz 1981-. [o.e. PvZ]

I, *Alexandrien. Kulturgegnungen dreier Jahrtausende im Schmelztiegel einer mediterranen Grossstadt*, by N. Hinske. 1981.

II, *Das römisch-byzantinische Ägypten.* Akten des internationalen Symposions 26.-30. September 1978 in Trier. 1984.

III, *Corpus of Mosaics from Egypt* I, by W.A. Daszewski. 1985.

IV, see *P.Neph.*

V, not yet published

VI, *Der Sarg der Teüris, eine Studie zum Totenglauben im römischen Ägypten*, by D. Kurth. 1990.

Aegyptus, Pubblicazioni, Serie Scientifica. Milan 1924-1938. (Pubblicazioni dell'Università Cattolica del Sacro Cuore, Contributi, Ser. III).

I, see *P.Mil.* I.1, 1st ed.

II, *Menandro*, by G. Capovilla. 1924.

III, *Raccolta di scritti in onore di G. Lumbroso.* 1925.

IV, *Testi e commenti concernenti l'antica Alessandria (= glossario Lumbroso)*, ed. E. Breccia, A. Calderini, G. Ghedini et al. Parts 1-3. 1934-1938.

V, *Atti del IV Congresso Internazionale di Papirologia, Firenze, 28 aprile-2 maggio 1935.* 1936. [Rp. CG]

Am.Stud.Pap. = *American Studies in Papyrology.* New Haven, Toronto, Las Palmas, Missoula, Chico, Decatur, Atlanta 1966-. (American Society of Papyrologists).

I, *Essays in Honor of C. Bradford Welles*, ed. A.E. Samuel. 1966. [o.e. SP]

II, see *P.Yale* I.

III, *Inventory of Compulsory Services in Ptolemaic and Roman Egypt*, by N. Lewis. 1968. [o.p.] See now N. Lewis, *The Compulsory Public Services of Roman Egypt.* Florence 1982. (Pap.Flor. XI).

IV, *The Taxes in Grain in Ptolemaic Egypt: Granary Receipts from Diospolis Magna, 164-88 B.C.*, by Z.M. Packman. 1968. [o.e. SP]

V, *Euripides Papyri* I, *Texts from Oxyrhynchus*, by B.E. Donovan. 1969. [o.e. SP]

VI, see *P.Mich.* X.

VII, *Proceedings of the Twelfth International Congress of Papyrology, Ann Arbor, Michigan, 12-17 August 1968*, ed. D.H. Samuel. 1970. [o.p.]

VIII, *The Ptolemaic and Roman Idios Logos*, by P.R. Swarney. 1970. [o.p.]

IX, see *P.Mich.* XI.

X, see *O.Ont.Mus.* I.

XI, *The Town Councils of Roman Egypt*, by A.K. Bowman. 1971. [o.p.]

XII, *The Four Greek Hymns of Isidorus and the Cult of Isis*, by V.F. Vanderlip. 1972. [o.e. SP]

XIII, *Greek Terms for Roman Institutions: A Lexicon and Analysis*, by H.J. Mason. 1974. [o.e. SP]

XIV, see *P.Mich.* XII.

XV, see *O.Ont.Mus.* II.

XVI, *Chester Beatty Biblical Papyri IV and V*, by A. Pietersma. 1977. [o.e. SP]

XVII, see *P.Wash.Univ.* I

XVIII, *Imperial Estates in Egypt*, by G.M. Parássoglou. Las Palmas 1978. [o.e. AMH]

XIX, *Status Declarations in Roman Egypt*, by C.A. Nelson. Las Palmas 1978. [o.e. AMH]

XX, see *P.Col.* VII.

XXI, *Le Nome Hermopolite: toponymes et sites*, by Marie Drew-Bear. Missoula 1979. [o.e. SP]

XXII, see *P.Mich.* XIV.

XXIII, *Proceedings of the Sixteenth International Congress of Papyrology*, ed. R.S. Bagnall, G.M. Browne, A.E. Hanson and L. Koenen. Chico 1981. [o.e. SP]

XXIV, see *P.Yale* II.

XXV, *Register of Oxyrhynchites*, 30 B.C.-A.D. 96, by B.W. Jones and J.E.G. Whitehorne. 1983. [o.e. SP]

XXVI, *Saite and Persian Demotic Cattle Documents, A Study in Legal Forms and Principles in Ancient Egypt*, by E. Cruz-Uribe. 1985. [o.e. SP]

XXVII, *Grundlagen des koptischen Satzbaus*, by H.J. Polotsky. 1987. (Half-title misnumbered 28, corrected on title-page verso.) [o.e. SP]

XXVIII, see *P.Col.* VIII.

XXIX, *Grundlagen des koptischen Satzbaus, zweite Hälfte*, by H.J. Polotsky. 1990. [o.e. SP]

XXX, see *P.Mich.* XVI.

XXXI, *Ptocheia or Odysseus in Disguise at Troy (P.Köln 245)*, Edition and Commentary by M.G. Parca. 1991. [o.e. SP]

BASP Suppl. = *Bulletin of the American Society of Papyrologists*: Supplements. Published irregularly by the Society, 1973- . [o.e. SP]

1, *Checklist of Editions of Greek Papyri and Ostraca*, 2nd ed., by J.F. Oates, R.S. Bagnall, W.H. Willis. 1978.

2, *Regnal Formulas in Byzantine Egypt*, by R.S. Bagnall, K.A. Worp. 1979.

3, *Abbreviations in Greek Literary Papyri and Ostraca*, by K. McNamee. 1981.

4, *Checklist of Editions of Greek Papyri and Ostraca*, 3rd ed., by J.F. Oates, R.S. Bagnall, W.H. Willis, K.A. Worp. 1985.

5, *Currency and Inflation in Fourth Century Egypt*, by R.S. Bagnall. 1985.

6, *The Production and Use of Vegetable Oils in Ptolemaic Egypt*, by D.B. Sandy. 1989.

7, *Checklist of Editions of Greek and Latin Papyri, Ostraca and Tablets*, 4th ed., by J.F. Oates, R.S. Bagnall, W.H. Willis, K.A. Worp. 1992.

Coll.Hellen. = *Collectanea Hellenistica*. Brussels 1989- . (Koninklijke Academie voor Wetenschappen, Letteren en Schone Kunsten van België, Klassieke Studies, Hellenisme, I-). [o.e. ARB]

I, *The Judaean-Syrian-Egyptian Conflict of 103-101 B.C., a Multilingual Dossier Concerning a "War of Sceptres,"* ed. by E. van 't Dack, W. Clarysse, G. Cohen, J. Quaegebeur and J.K. Winnicki. 1989.

II, see *P.Petr.*[2].

Estud.Pap. = Estudis de Papirologia i Filologia Bíblica. Barcelona 1991-.

1, *The Funerary Papyrus Palau Rib. nr. inv. 450*, ed. C. Sturtewagen. 1991.

2, *Il lessico latino nel greco d'Egitto*, 2nd ed., by S. Daris. 1991.

Graeco-Roman Memoirs, Egypt Exploration Society. London, 1898- .

1, see *P.Oxy.* I.

2, see *P.Oxy.* II.

3, see *P.Fay.*

4, see *P.Tebt*. I.
5, see *P.Oxy*. III.
6, see *P.Oxy*. IV.
7, see *P.Hib*. I.
8, see *P.Oxy*. V.
9, see *P.Oxy*. VI.
10, see *P.Oxy*. VII.
11, see *P.Oxy*. VIII.
12, see *P.Oxy*. IX.
13, see *P.Oxy*. X.
14, see *P.Oxy*. XI.
15, see *P.Oxy*. XII.
16, see *P.Oxy*. XIII.
17, see *P.Oxy*. XIV.
18, see *P.Oxy*. XV.
19, see *P.Oxy*. XVI.
20, see *P.Oxy*. XVII.
21, see *O.Bodl*. I.
22, *Two Theocritus Papyri*, ed. A.S. Hunt and J. Johnson. 1930.
23, see *P.Tebt*. III, Part I.
24, *Greek Shorthand Manuals*, ed. H.J.M. Milne. 1934. (III, Corpora)
25, see *P.Tebt*. III, Part II.
26, see *P.Oxy*. XVIII.
27, see *P.Oxy*. XIX.
28, see *P.Ant*. I.
29, see *P.Oxy*. XX.
30, see *P.Oxy*. XXI.
31, see *P.Oxy*. XXII.
32, see *P.Hib*. II.
33, see *O.Bodl*. II.
34, see *P.Oxy*. XXIII.
35, see *P.Oxy*. XXIV.
36, see *P.Oxy*. XXV.
37, see *P.Ant*. II.
38, see *P.Oxy*. XXVI.
39, see *P.Oxy*. XXVII.
40, see *P.Oxy*. XXVIII.
41, see *P.Oxy*. XXIX.
42, see *P.Herm*.

43, see *O.Bodl.* III, *Indexes.*
44, see *P.Oxy.* XXX.
45, see *P.Oxy.* XXXI.
46, see *P.Oxy.* XXXII.
47, see *P.Ant.* III.
48, see *P.Oxy.* XXXIII.
49, see *P.Oxy.* XXXIV.
50, see *P.Oxy.* XXXV.
51, see *P.Oxy.* XXXVI.
52, see *P.Tebt.* II, reprint 1970.
53, see *P.Oxy.* XXXVII.
54, see *P.Oxy.* XXXVIII.
55, see *P.Oxy.* XXXIX.
56, see *P.Oxy.* XL.
57, see *P.Oxy.* XLI.
58, see *P.Oxy.* XLII.
59, *Location List of the Oxyrhynchus Papyri*, by R.A. Coles. 1974.
60, see *P.Oxy.* XLIII.
61, see Sec. VII, Proceedings, no. XIV.
62, see *P.Oxy.* XLIV.
63, see *P.Oxy.* XLV.
64, see *P.Tebt.* IV.
65, see *P.Oxy.* XLVI.
66, see *P.Oxy.* XLVII.
67, see *P.Oxy.* XLVIII.
68, see *P.Turner.*
69, see *P.Oxy.* XLIX.
70, see *P.Oxy.* L.
71, see *P.Oxy.* LI.
72, see *P.Oxy.* LII.
73, see *P.Oxy.* LIII.
74, see *P.Oxy.* LIV.
75, see *P.Oxy.* LV.
76, see *P.Oxy.* LVI.
77, see *P.Oxy.* LVII.
78, see *P.Oxy.* LVIII.

MPER = *Mittheilungen aus der Sammlung der Papyrus Erzherzog Rainer*, ed. J. Karabacek. Vienna. A publication of various articles, some concerned with Greek papyri. [MF 2.40-44]

I, 1887.

II-III, 1887.

IV, 1888.

V, 1892.

VI, 1897.

MPER N.S. = *Mitteilungen aus der Papyrussammlung der Österreichischen Nationalbibliothek in Wien*, Neue Serie.

I, *Griechische literarische Papyri* I, ed. H. Gerstinger, H. Oellacher, K. Vogel. Vienna 1932. [MF 2.82]

II, *Koptische Pergamente theologischen Inhalts*, ed. W. Till. Vienna 1934. [MF 2.83]

III, *Griechische literarische Papyri* II, ed. H. Oellacher, with an index to Parts I and II by H. Gerstinger and P. Sanz. Vienna 1939. [MF 2.84]

IV, *Griechische literarische Papyri christlichen Inhaltes* I (*Biblica, Väterschriften und Verwandtes*), ed. P. Sanz. Vienna 1946. [o.e. RHR]

V, *Akten des VIII. Internationalen Kongresses für Papyrologie, Wien 1955*. Vienna 1956. [o.e. RHR]

VI, *Aegypter und Amazonen (Pap.dem.Vindob. 6165 und 6165A)*, ed. A. Volten. Vienna 1962. [o.e. ÖNB]

VII, *Aus der Vorgeschichte der Papyrussammlung der Oesterreichischen Nationalbibliothek* (Letters of T. Graf, J. von Karabacek, Erzherzog Rainer and others), ed. H. Hunger. Vienna 1962. [o.e. ÖNB]

VIII, *Der Kampf um den Panzer des Inaros (Papyrus Krall)*, ed. E. Bresciani. Vienna 1964. [o.e. ÖNB]

IX, *Koptische Papyri theologischen Inhalts*, ed. T. Orlandi. Vienna 1974. [o.e. ÖNB]

X, *From the Contents of the Libraries of the Suchos Temples in the Fayum, Part I: A medical Book from Crocodilopolis, P.Vindob. D. 6257*, ed. E.A.E. Reymond. Vienna 1976. [o.e. ÖNB]

XI, *From the Contents of the Libraries of the Suchos Temples in the Fayum, Part II: From Ancient Egyptian Hermetic Writings*, ed. E.A.E. Reymond. Vienna 1977. [o.e. ÖNB]

XII, *Prosopographia Arsinoitica I, S.VI-VIII*, by J.M. Diethart. Vienna 1980.

XIII, *Medizinische Rezepte und Verwandtes*, ed. H. Harrauer and P.J. Sijpesteijn. Vienna 1981. [o.e. ÖNB]

XIV, *Koranfragmente auf Pergament aus der Papyrussammlung der Österreichischen Nationalbibliothek*, ed. H. Loebenstein. Vienna 1982. [o.e. ÖNB]

XV, see *P.Rain.Unterricht.*

XVI, *Notarsunterschriften im Byzantinischen Ägypten*, by J.M. Diethart and K.A. Worp. Vienna 1986. Separate volume of plates. [o.e. ÖNB]

XVII, Not yet published

XVIII, *Neue Texte und Dokumentation zum koptisch-Unterricht*, by M. Hasitzka. Vienna 1990. Separate volume of plates. Nos. 1-332. [o.e. ÖNB]

XIX, *Bericht über das 1. Wiener Symposion für Papyrusrestaurierung*, ed. H. Harrauer. Vienna 1985. [o.e. AHN]

XX, *Das Amt des* ἀπαιτητής *in Ägypten*, by B. Palme. Vienna 1989. [o.e. ÖNB]

XXI, *Coptic Theological Papyri II, Edition, Commentary, Translation*, with an appendix: *The Docetic Jesus*, by I. Gardner. Vienna 1988. Separate volume of plates. [o.e. ÖNB]

Pap.Brux. = *Papyrologica Bruxellensia*. Brussels 1962- . (Fondation Égyptologique Reine Élisabeth).

I, see *P.Iand.inv.653.*

II, *Les Titulatures impériales dans les papyrus, les ostraca et les inscriptions d'Égypte (30 a.C.-284 p.C.)*, by P. Bureth. 1964. [o.e. FERE]

III, *La Sitométrie dans les archives de Zénon*, by T. Reekmans. 1966. [o.e. FERE]

IV, *Reports of Proceedings in Papyri*, by R.A. Coles. 1966. [o.e. FERE]

V, *Le Bordereau d'ensemencement dans l'Égypte ptolémaïque*, by P. Vidal-Naquet. 1967. [o.e. FERE]

VI, *Recherches de papyrologie littéraire I, Concordances*, by P. Mertens. 1968. [o.e. FERE]

VII, see *P.Alex.Giss.*

VIII, *Epimerismos*, by G. Poethke. 1969. [o.e. FERE]

IX, *Le Stratège du nome*, by N. Hohlwein. 1969. [o.e. FERE] (Rp. of articles of 1924-1925)

X, *Les Ressources et les activités économiques des églises en Égypte du IVe au VIIIe siècle*, by E. Wipszycka. 1972. [o.e. FERE]

XI, *Gli strateghi dell'Arsinoites in epoca romana*, by G. Bastianini. 1972. [o.e. FERE]

XII, *L. Domitius Domitianus*, by J. Schwartz. 1975. [o.e. FERE]

XIII, *Papyrus littéraires grecs*, by J. Lenaerts. 1977. [o.e. FERE]

XIV, *Greeks and Egyptians*, by J.W.B. Barns. 1978. [o.e. FERE]

XV, see *P.Hombert.*

XVI-XIX, *Actes du XVe Congrès International de Papyrologie*, ed. J. Bingen and G. Nachtergael. [o.e. FERE]

XVI, Part I, *The Terms Recto and Verso and the Anatomy of the Papyrus Roll*, by E.G. Turner. 1978.

XVII, Part II, *Textes inédits.* 1979. (= *P.Congr.XV*).

XVIII, Part III, *Problèmes généraux, Papyrologie littéraire.* 1979.

XIX, Part IV, *Papyrologie documentaire.* 1980.

XX, *L'Arpentage par espèces dans l'Égypte ptolémaïque d'après les papyrus grecs*, by H. Cuvigny. 1985. [o.e. FERE]

XXI, see *P.Erasm.* I.

XXII, *Les Titulatures des empereurs romains dans les documents en langue égyptienne*, by J.-C. Grenier. 1989. [o.e. FERE]

XXIII, *Papyrus in Classical Antiquity, a Supplement*, by N. Lewis. 1989. A supplement to N. Lewis, *Papyrus in Classical Antiquity* (Oxford 1974).

XXIV, see *C.Ord.Ptol.*, supplement (III, Corpora)

XXV, *Magica varia*, five miscellaneous texts ed. by W.M. Brashear with contributions by A. Bülow-Jacobsen. 1991. [o.e. FERE]

XXVI, *Sigla and Select Marginalia in Greek Literary Papyri*, by K. McNamee. 1992. [o.e. FERE]

Pap.Castr. = *Papyrologica Castroctaviana*. Barcelona 1967- .

I, *El papiro en los padres grecolatinos*, ed. J. O'Callaghan. 1967. [o.e. PIB]

II, *Un nuovo frammento della Prima Lettera di Pietro*, ed. S. Daris. 1967. [o.e. PIB]

III, *Il lessico latino nel greco d'Egitto*, by S. Daris. 1971. Second edition, Barcelona 1991 (*Estudis de Papirologia i Filologia bíblica* 2).

IV, *Das Markusevangelium saïdisch*, ed. H. Quecke. 1972. [o.e. PIB]

V, *L'Evoluzione della scrittura nei papiri greci del Vecchio Testamento*, by A. Leone. 1975. [o.e. PIB]

VI, *Das Lukasevangelium saïdisch*, ed. H. Quecke. 1977. [o.e. PIB]

VII, *Michigan Coptic Texts*, ed. G.M. Browne. 1979. [o.e. PIB]

VIII, *Griffith's Old Nubian Lectionary*, by G.M. Browne. 1982.

IX, *Gli Accenti nei papiri greci biblici*, by A. Biondi. 1983.

X, *Chrysostomus Nubianus: An Old Nubian Version of Ps. Chrysostomus, "In Venerabilem Crucem Sermo"*, by G.M. Browne. 1984.

XI, *Das Johannesevangelium saïdisch*, ed. H. Quecke. 1984.

XII, *Gli Animali da trasporto nell'Egitto greco, romano e bizantino*, by A. Leone. 1988.

Pap.Colon. = *Papyrologica Coloniensia*, Sonderreihe of the series Wissenschaftliche Abhandlungen der Arbeitsgemeinschaft für Forschung des Landes Nordrhein-Westfalen. Cologne and Opladen, 1964- .

I, *Der Psalmenkommentar von Tura, Quaternio IX*, ed. A. Kehl. 1964. [o.e. WDV]

II, *Demotische und koptische Texte*, ed. E. Lüddeckens, A.M. Kropp, A. Hermann, M. Weber. 1968. [o.e. WDV]

III, *The Ptolemaic Papyri of Homer*, by S. West. 1967. [o.e. WDV]

IV, see *P.Petaus*.

V, *Katalog Alexandrinischer Kaisermünzen der Sammlung des Instituts für Altertumskunde der Universität zu Köln*,

  Bd. 1: *Augustus-Trajan (Nr. 1-740)*, by A. Geissen. 1974. [o.e. WDV]

  Bd.2: *Hadrian-Antoninus Pius (Nr. 741-1994)*. 1978. [o.e. WDV]

  Bd.3: *Marc Aurel-Gallienus (Nr. 1995-3014)*. 1982. [o.e. WDV]

  Bd.4: *Claudius Gothicus-Bleimünzen (Nr. 3015-3627)*, by A. Geissen, W. Weiser. 1983. [o.e. WDV]

  Bd.5: *Indices zu den Bänden 1 bis 4*, by W. Weiser. 1983. [o.e. WDV]

VI, *The Epistrategos in Ptolemaic and Roman Egypt*, by J.D. Thomas.

  Part I: *The Ptolemaic Epistrategos*. 1975. [o.e. WDV]

  Part II: *The Roman Epistrategos*. 1982. [o.e. WDV]

VII, see *P.Köln*.

VIII, see *P.Soter*.

IX, *Kölner Ägyptische Papyri* I, ed. D. Kurth, H.-J. Thissen and M.
Weber. 1980. [o.e. WDV]

X, *Dionysios Scytobrachion*, ed. J.S. Rusten. 1982. [o.e. WDV]

XI, *Katalog der Bithynischen Münzen der Sammlung des Instituts für
Altertumskunde der Universität zu Köln*, Bd. 1: *Nikaia*, by W.
Weiser. 1983. [o.e. WDV]

XII, *Le Papyrus inv. 5853 de l'Université de Cologne: un contrat de
mariage écrit en caractères hébraiques*, ed. C. Sirat, P. Cauderlier,
M. Dukan and M. Friedman. 1986. [o.e. WDV]

XIII, see *Pap.Agon.*

XIV, *Der Kölner Mani-Kodex*, ed. L. Koenen and C. Römer, 1988.
[o.e. WDV]

XV, see *P.Bub.*

XVI, see *Suppl. Mag.* (III, Corpora).

XVII, *Abrasax: Ausgewählte Papyri religiösen und magischen Inhalts*,
by R. Merkelbach and M. Totti. Part 1, 1990; part 2, 1991. [o.e.
WDV]

XVIII, see *P.Wash.Univ.* II.

XIX, *Two Greek Magical Papyri in the National Museum of
Antiquities in Leiden*, ed. R.W. Daniel. 1991. [o.e. WDV]

Pap.Flor. = *Papyrologica Florentina*. Florence. 1976- .

I, see *P.Laur.* I.

II, see *P.Laur.* II.

III, *Euripide, Erretteo*, Introduzione, testo e commento by P. Carrara.
1977. [o.e. LGF]

IV, *Demosthenis fragmenta in papyris et membranis servata* (pars
prima), by B. Hausmann. 1978. [Rp. Diss. Leipzig 1921; LFG]

V, see *P.Laur.* III.

VI, see *P.Genova* II.

VII, *Miscellanea Papyrologica*, ed. R. Pintaudi. 1980. [o.e. LGF]

VIII, *Demosthenis fragmenta in papyris et membranis servata*, (pars
secunda and pars tertia, appendice di aggiornamento), by B.
Hausmann 1981. [Rp. Diss. Leipzig 1921; LGF].

IX, *I Centri abitati dell' Ossirinchite*, by P. Pruneti. 1981. [o.e. LGF]

X, *Sofocle, Ichneutae*, Introduzione, testo critico, interpretazione e
commento, by E. V. Maltese. 1982. [o.e. LFG]

XI, *The Compulsory Public Services of Roman Egypt*, by N. Lewis.
1982. [o.e. LGF]

XII, see *P.Laur.* IV.

XII Supplement, *Papiri greci e latini a Firenze. Secoli iii a.C.-viii d.C. Biblioteca Medicea Laurenziana. Catalogo della mostra maggio-giugno 1983*, by R. Pintaudi. [o.e. LGF]

XIII, see *P.Laur.* V.

XIV, see *O.Cair.*

XV, *Strategi and Royal Scribes of Roman Egypt, Chronological List and Index*, by G. Bastianini and J.E.G. Whitehorne. 1987. [o.e. LGF]

XVI, see *P.Prag.* I.

XVII, see *O.Ashm.Shelt.*

XVIII, see *T.Varie.*

XIX, *Miscellanea papyrologica in occasione del bicentenario dell'edizione della Charta Borgiana*, ed. M. Capasso, G. Messeri Savorelli, R. Pintaudi. 2 vols. 1990. [o.e. LGF]

XX, see *P.Genova* III.

XXI, *Studia Hellenistica*, scripta minora by E. Livrea, in two parts. 1991. [o.e. LGF]

XXII, see *P.Brook.*

XXIII, see *C.Epist.Lat.*

Pap.Heid. = *Veröffentlichungen aus der Heidelberger Papyrussammlung.*

I, *Die Septuaginta-Papyri*, ed. A. Deissmann. Heidelberg 1905. [MF 2.31]

II, *Acta Pauli aus der Heidelberger koptischen Papyrus-Handschrift Nr. 1*, ed. C. Schmidt. Leipzig 1904. [MF 2.32]

III, *Papyri Schott-Reinhardt* I, ed. C.H. Becker. Heidelberg 1906. Greek texts reprinted as *SB I 5638-5655. [MF 2.33]

IV, *Griechisch literarische Papyri* I, *Ptolemäische Homerfragmente*, ed. G.A. Gerhard. Heidelberg 1911. [o.e. CWV]

N.F. I, *Zum Drogenhandel im islamischen Aegypten* ed. A. Dietrich. Heidelberg 1954. [o.e. CWV]

N.F. II, see *P.Heid.* I.

N.F. III, see *P.Heid.* III.

N.F. IV, *Die demotischen Gebelên-Urkunden der Heidelberger Papyrussammlung*, ed. U. Kaplony-Heckel. Heidelberg 1964. Nos. 1-42. [o.e. CWV]

N.F. V, see *P.Heid.* IV.

N.F. VI, see *P.Heid.* V.

Pap.Lugd.Bat. = *Papyrologica Lugduno-Batava*. Leiden 1941-.

I, see *P.Warr*.

II, see *P.Vindob.Bosw*.

III, See *P.Oxf*.

IV, *De Herodoti reliquiis in papyris et membranis aegyptiis servatis*, by A.H.R.E. Paap. 1948. [MF 2.58]

V, *Recherches sur le recensement dans l'Égypte romaine (P.Bruxelles inv. E.7616)*, ed. M. Hombert and C. Préaux. 1952. [MF 2.59] Now reprinted as *P.Brux*. I 1-18.

VI, see *P.Fam.Tebt*.

VII, *Les Noms propres du P.Bruxelles inv. E.7616. Essai d'interprétation*, by J. Vergote. 1954. [MF 2.61]

VIII, *Nomina Sacra in the Greek Papyri of the First Five Centuries A.D.*, by A.H.R.E. Paap. 1959. [MF 2.62]

IX, *Marriage and Matrimonial Property in Ancient Egypt*, by P.W. Pestman. 1961. [MF 2.63]

X, *Aeschylus' Dictyulci*, ed. M. Werre-de Haas. 1961. [MF 2.64]

XI, see *P.Vindob.Sijp*.

XII, *Penthemeros Certificates in Graeco-Roman Egypt*, by P.J. Sijpesteijn. 1964. [o.e. EJB]

XIII, see *P.Select*.

XIV, *Studia papyrologica varia*, ed. E. Boswinkel, P.W. Pestman, P.J. Sijpesteijn. 1965. [o.e. EJB]

XV, *Chronologie égyptienne d'après les textes démotiques: 332 av. J.-C.-453 ap.J.C.*, by P.W. Pestman. 1967. [o.e. EJB]

XVI, see *P.Wisc*. I.

XVII, see *P.David*.

XVIII, *The Xenophon Papyri (Anabasis, Cyropaedia, Cynegeticus, De Vectigalibus)*, by A.H.R.E. Paap. 1970. [o.e. EJB]

XIX, see *P.Batav*.

XX, see *P.Zen.Pestm*.

XXI, *A Guide to the Zenon Archive*, ed. P.W. Pestman et al. 1981. 2 vols. [o.e. EJB]

XXII, see *P.Dion*.

XXIII, *Textes et études de papyrologie grecque, démotique et copte*, ed. P.W. Pestman. Leiden 1985. Besides studies, this volume publishes one ostracon in Greek (pp.7-8), 10 in Demotic. [o.e. EJB]

XXIV, *The Eponymous Priests of Ptolemaic Egypt*, by W. Clarysse and G. van der Veken, with S.P. Vleeming. 1983. [o.e. EJB]

XXV, see *P.Leid.Inst.*

Pap.Texte Abh. = *Papyrologische Texte und Abhandlungen*, ed. L. Koenen, R. Merkelbach, D. Hagedorn and R. Kassel. Bonn 1968- .

I, *Didymos der Blinde, Kommentar zu Hiob (Tura-Papyrus)*, Teil I, ed. A. Henrichs. 1968. [o.e. RH]

II, *Didymos der Blinde, Kommentar zu Hiob (Tura-Papyrus)*, Teil II, ed. A. Henrichs. 1968. [o.e. RH]

III, *Didymos der Blinde, Kommentar zu Hiob (Tura-Papyrus)*, Teil III, ed. U. Hagedorn, D. Hagedorn, L. Koenen. 1968. [o.e. RH]

IV, *Didymos der Blinde, Psalmenkommentar*, Teil II, ed. M. Gronewald. 1968. [o.e. RH]

V, *Der Septuaginta-Text des Buches Daniel*, etc., ed. A. Geissen. 1968. [o.e. RH]

VI, *Didymos der Blinde, Psalmenkommentar*, Teil IV, ed. M. Gronewald. 1969. [o.e. RH]

VII, *Didymos der Blinde, Psalmenkommentar*, Teil I, ed. L. Doutreleau, A. Gesché, M. Gronewald. 1969. [o.e. RH]

VIII, *Didymos der Blinde, Psalmenkommentar*, Teil III, ed. M. Gronewald. 1969. [o.e. RH]

IX, *Didymos der Blinde, Kommentar zum Ecclesiastes (Tura-Papyrus)*, Teil VI, ed. G. Binder and L. Liesenborghs. 1969. [o.e. RH]

X, *Der Septuaginta Text des Buches Daniel, Kap. 1-2 (Pap. 967)*, ed. W. Hamm. 1969. [o.e. RH]

XI, *Die Aegyptenreise des Germanicus*, by D.G. Weingärtner. 1969. [o.e. RH]

XII, *Didymos der Blinde, Psalmenkommetar*, Teil V, ed. M. Gronewald. 1970. [o.e. RH]

XIII, *Didymos der Blinde, Kommentar zum Eccesiastes (Tura-Papyrus)*, Teil III, ed. J. Kramer. 1970. [o.e. RH]

XIV, *Die Phoinikika des Lollianos: Fragmente eines neuen griechischen Romans*, ed. A. Henrichs. 1972. [o.e. RH]

XV, *Der griechische Text des Buches Ezechiel (Pap. 967)*, ed. L.G. Jahn. 1972. [o.e. RH]

XVI, *Didymos der Blinde, Kommentar zum Ecclesiastes (Tura-Papyrus)*, Teil IV, ed. J. Kramer and B. Krebber. 1972. [o.e. RH]

XVII, see *P.Cair.Mich.*, pt I.

XVIII, see *P.Cair.Mich.*, pt. II.

XIX, see *P.Coll.Youtie* I.

XX, see *P.Coll.Youtie* II.

XXI, *Der Septuaginta Text des Buches Daniel Kap. 3-4 nach d. Kölner Teil d. Papyrus 967*, ed. W. Hamm. 1977. [o.e. RH]

XXII, *Didymos der Blinde, Kommentar zum Ecclesiastes (Turapapyrus)*, Teil II, ed. M. Gronewald. 1977. [o.e. RH]

XXIII, see *P.Sakaon.*

XXIV, *Didymos der Blinde, Kommentar zum Ecclesiastes (Tura-Papyrus)*, Teil V, ed. G. Binder and M. Gronewald. 1979. [o.e. RH]

XXV, *Didymos der Blinde, Kommentar zum Ecclesiastes (Tura-Papyrus)*, Teil I.1, ed. G. Binder and L. Liesenborghs. 1979. [o.e. RH]

XXVI, *Didymos der Blinde, Kommentar zum Ecclesiastes (Tura-Papyrus)*, Teil I.2, ed. G. Binder. 1982. [o.e. RH]

XXVII, *Three Rolls of the Early Septuagint: Genesis and Deuteronomy*, by Z. Aly, with preface, introduction and notes by L. Koenen. 1980. [o.e. RH]

XXVIII, see *P.Ups.Frid.*

XXIX, see *P.Haun.* II.

XXX, *Glossaria bilinguia in Papyris et Membranis reperta*, ed. J. Kramer. 1983. [o.e. RH]

XXXI, see *P.Hamb.* III.

XXXII, *Die Lehre des Anchscheschonqi (P. BM 10508)*, ed. H.-J. Thissen. 1984 [o.e. RH]

XXXIII, pt. 1, *Didymos der Blinde, Kommentar zu Hiob 12, 1-16, 8a*, ed. U. Hagedorn, D. Hagedorn and L. Koenen. 1985. [o.e. RH]

XXXIV, *Kleine Texte aus dem Tura-Fund*, ed. B. Kramer. 1985. [o.e. RH]

XXXV, *Der Kölner Mani-Kodex: Abbildungen und diplomatischer Text*, ed. L. Koenen and C. Römer. 1985. [o.e. RH]

XXXVI, see *P.Haun.* III.

XXXVII, *Studi Cercidei (P.Oxy. 1082)*, ed. E. Livrea. 1986. [o.e. RH]

XXXVIII, see *P.Freib.* IV.

XXXIX, see *P.Diog.*

XL, *Management and Investment on Estates in Roman Egypt during the Early Empire*, by D.P. Kehoe. 1992. [o.e. RH]

Princ.Stud.Pap. = *Princeton University Studies in Papyrology*, vols. I-VI. 1936-1949. [PUP]

I, see *P.Princ*. II.

II, *Taxation in Egypt from Augustus to Diocletian*, by S.L. Wallace. 1938.

III, see *P.Princ.Scheide*.

IV, see *P.Princ*. III.

V, *Currency in Roman and Byzantine Egypt*, by L.C. West and A.C. Johnson. 1944.

VI, *Byzantine Egypt. Economic Studies*, by A.C. Johnson and L.C. West. 1949.

Publ.Soc.Fouad = *Publications de la Société Fouad I* (later *Égyptienne*) de *Papyrologie, Textes et Documents*. Cairo 1931-1951.

I, see *P.Enteux*.

II, *Un livre d'écolier du IIIe siècle avant J.-C.*, ed. O. Guéraud and P. Jouguet. 1938. [MF 2.90]

III, see *P.Fouad*.

IV, *I resti dell'XI libro del* περὶ φύσεως *di Epicuro*, ed. A. Vogliano. 1940. [MF 2.92]

V, see *P.Cair.Zen*. V.

VI, *Demotic Ostraka*, ed. G. Mattha. 1945. [MF 2.93]

VII, see *P.Phil*.

VIII, see *P.Fuad Univ*.

IX, *Entretien d'Origène avec Héraclide et les évêques ses collègues*, ed. J. Scherer. 1949. [MF 2.96]

X, *Les Inscriptions grecques du temple de Hatshepsout à Deir el Bahari*, ed. A. Bataille. 1951. [MF 2.97]

Publ.Sorb.Pap. = Publications de la Sorbonne, Série "Papyrologie", Université de Paris IV, Paris Sorbonne.

I, *Catalogue des papyrus juifs et chrétiens*, by J. van Haelst. 1976.

II, *OIKIA, Le vocabulaire de la maison privée en Égypte d'après les papyrus grecs*, by G. Husson. 1983.

III, see *P.Thmouis* I.

Ric.Pap. = *Ricerca Papirologica*. Messina, 1992-.

1, see *Oroscopi* (III, Corpora)

2, *Alle origini delle abbreviature latine. Una prima ricognizione (I secolo a.C. - IV secolo d.C.)*, by N. Giove'Marchioli. 1992. [o.e. ES]

Schr.Heid. = *Schriften des Papyrusinstitut Heidelberg.* Berlin and Leipzig, Walter de Gruyter, 1920-1922. (See also Stud.Heid. below).

I, *Vom göttlichen Fluidum nach ägyptischer Anschauung*, by F. Preisigke. 1920.

II, *Ein bisher unbeachtetes Dokument zur Frage nach dem Wesen der* κατοχή *im Serapeum von Memphis*, ed. K. Sethe. 1921.

III, *Das Signalment in den Papyrusurkunden*, by J. Hasebroek. 1921.

IV, see *O.Berl.*

V, *Das Verhältnis der griechischen und ägyptischen Texte in den zweisprachigen Dekreten von Rosette und Kanopus*, by W. Spiegelberg. 1922.

VI, *Die Gotteskraft der frühchristlichen Zeit*, by F. Preisigke. 1922.

SPP, see *Stud.Pal.*

Stud.Amst. = *Studia Amstelodamensia ad epigraphicam, ius antiquum et papyrologicam pertinentia.* Amsterdam 1972-76,1990- , Zutphen 1976-86.

I, See *P.Vindob.Worp.*

II, *Index of Articles, Volumes 1-50 of Aegyptus*, by S.M.E. van Lith. 1974. [o.e. AMH]

III, *The Charm of Legal History*, by H. van den Brink. 1974. [o.e. AMH]

IV, see *P.Vindob.Sal.*

V, see *P.Theon.*

VI, see *P.Vindob.Tand.*

VII, see *P.Herm.Landl.*

VIII, *Chronological Systems of Byzantine Egypt*, by R.S. Bagnall and K.A. Worp. 1978. [o.e. TPC]

IX, see *O.Amst.*

X, see *P.Mich.* XIII.

XI, see *P.Wisc.* II.

XII, see *P.Charite.*

XIII, *Die Haftung der Schiffer im griechischen und römischen Recht*, by A.J.M. Meyer-Termeer. 1978. [o.e. TPC]

XIV, see *P.Amst.* I.

XV, *Studien zur allgemeinen Rechtslehre des Gaius*, by H. Wagner. 1978. [o.e. TPC]

XVI, *Nouvelles inscriptions de Phrygie*, by T. Drew-Bear. 1978. [o.e. TPC]

XVII, see *P.Customs.*

XVIII, *Gaius Noster: Plaidoyer pour Gaius*, by O. Stanojevic. 1989.

XIX, see *P.Mich.* XV.

XX, *Tyriaion en Cabalide: épigraphie et géographie historique*, by C. Naour. 1980. [o.e. TPC]

XXI, *The Roman Law of Succession in the Letters of Pliny the Younger* I, by J.W. Tellegen. 1982. [o.e. TPC]

XXII, *Testamentary Succession in the Constitutions of Diocletian*, by O.E. Tellegen-Couperus. 1982. [o.e. TPC]

XXIII, *Les triptyques de Transylvanie: études juridiques*, by G. Ciulei. 1983. [o.e. TPC]

XXIV, *Restaurierung von Papyrus und anderen Schriftträgern aus Ägypten*, by M. Fackelmann. 1985. [o.e. TPC]

XXV, *Error iuris nocet: Rechtsirrtum als Problem der Rechtsordnung*, I, *Rechtsirrtum in der griechischen Philosophie und im römischen Recht bis Justinian*, by L.C. Winkel. 1985. [o.e. TPC]

XXVI, see *P.Harr.* II.

XXVII, *Opera selecta*: *Études de droit romain et d'histoire du droit*, by H.R. Hoetink. 1986. [o.e. TPC]

XXVIII, *Nouvelle liste des gymnasiarques des métropoles de l'Égypte romaine*, by P.J. Sijpesteijn. 1986. [o.e. TPC]

XXIX, *Roman Imperial Titulature and Chronology, A.D. 235-284*, by M. Peachin. 1990. [o.e. JCG]

XXX, *Le Droit romain en Dacie*, by V. Sotropa. 1990. [o.e. JCG]

XXXI, *Food for Rome. The Legal Structure of the Transportation and Processing of Supplies for the Imperial Distributions in Rome and Constantinople*, by B. Sirks. 1991. [o.e. JCG]

Stud.Heid. = *Studien zur Epigraphik und Papyruskunde*, ed. F. Bilabel, vol. I (no more published). Leipzig, Dieterich'sche Verlagsbuchhandlung, 1927-1930. Planned as a resumption of Schr.Heid. (see above) but only three Studien were published, as follows:

1, *Die lateinischen Wörter und Namen in den griechischen Papyri*, by B. Meinersmann, 1927.

2, *Die Personennamen der Kopten* I (Untersuchungen), by G. Heuser. 1929. (Of the proposed Part II, Namenbuch, a first part was published as *Prosopographie von Ägypten*, IV: *Die Kopten*, by G. Heuser. Heidelberg 1938. (Quellen und Studien zur Geschichte und Kultur des Altertums und des Mittelalters, Reihe C: Hilfsbücher, Band 2.)

4, *Die semitischen Menschennamen in griechischen Inschriften und Papyri des vorderen Orients*, by H. Wuthnow. 1930.

Stud.Pal. (or SPP) = *Studien zur Palaeographie und Papyruskunde*, ed. C. Wessely. Leipzig 1901-1924. An approximately annual publication, issued irregularly, and miscellaneous in character. Vols. I-V, VII, VIII, X, XIII, XIV, XVII, XX and XXII include documentary texts.

I, Greek texts in: "Die griechischen Papyrusurkunden des Theresianums in Wien," ed. C. Wessely, nos. 1-4 (pp.1-5, no. 4 reprinted as *SB* III 6086); "Trois papyrus du musée Guimet trouvés à Antinoë," ed. S. de Ricci, nos. 1-3 (pp. 6-8). 1901. [MF 2.114 (with vols. II and IV); rp. AMH]

II, Greek texts in "Die jüngsten Volkszählungen und die ältesten Indictionen in Ägypten," ed. C. Wessely, nos. 1-3 and four others unnumbered (pp.26-35, no. 2 reprinted in vol. XXII 7). 1902. [MF 2.114 (with vols. I and IV); rp. AMH]

III, *Griechische Papyrusurkunden kleineren Formats* (*P.Kl.Form.* I), ed. C. Wessely. Nos. 1-701. 1904. [MF 2.115 (with VIII); rp. AMH]

*IV, Greek texts in: "Papyrus ptolémaïques," ed. S. de Ricci, nos. 1-3 (pp.53-57; no. 3 republished as *UPZ* II 158b); "Arsinoitische Verwaltungsurkunden vom Jahre 72/3 nach Chr.," ed. C. Wessely, reedition of *P.Lond.* II 260 and 261 adding Rainer fragment, with indices (pp.58-83); "Die Papyri der öffentlichen Sammlungen in Graz," ed. C. Wessely, full edition of descripta *P.Oxy.* II 368, III 603, 636, 647 and *P.Fay.* 153, 229, 260, 264, 322, 341 (pp. 114-21); Indices to vols. I, II and IV. 1905. [MF 2.114 (with vols. I and II); rp. AMH]

*V, *Corpus Papyrorum Hermopolitanorum* I (*C.P.Herm.*), ed. C. Wessely. Nos. 1-127. 1905. [MF 2.116; rp. AMH]

VI, *Kolotes und Menedemos: Texte und Untersuchungen zur Philosophen- und Literaturgeschichte*, ed. W. Crönert. 1906. [Rp. AMH]

*VII, *Demotische und griechische Texte auf Mumientäfelchen in der Sammlung der Papyrus Erzherzog Rainer*, ed. N. Reich. Nos. 1-19; 1-4, 9,12-15,17,19 have both Greek and Demotic; the Greek is reprinted in *SB* I (see *SB* II p.139 *s.n.* Reich). 1908. [Rp. AMH]

VIII, *Griechische Papyrusurkunden kleineren Formats* (*P.Kl.Form.* II), ed. C. Wessely. Nos. 702-1346, with indices to vols. III and VIII. 1908. [MF 2.115 (with vol. III); rp. AMH]

IX, *Griechische und koptische Texte theologischen Inhalts* I, ed. C. Wessely. Nos 1-54. 1909. [Rp. AMH]

X, *Griechische Texte zur Topographie Aegyptens*, ed. C. Wessely. Nos. 1-299. 1910. [MF 2.117; rp. AMH]

XI, *Griechische und koptische Texte theologischen Inhalts* II, ed. C. Wessely. Nos. 55-113. 1911. [Rp. AMH]

XII, *Griechische und koptische Texte theologischen Inhalts* III, ed. C. Wessely. Nos 114-192. 1912. [Rp. AMH]

*XIII, Greek texts in: "Sklaven-Prosangelie bei der Bibliotheke Enkteseon," ed. C. Wessely, three texts (pp.1-3; no. 3 = *P.Lond.* II 299 = *Chrest.Mitt.* 204); "Eine Urkunde aus dem 6. Konsulat des Kaisers Licinius," ed. Wessely (pp.6-7, reprinted as *SB* I 5810); "Das Ghetto von Apollinopolis Magna," ed. Wessely, ostraca nos. 1-20 (pp. 8-10; most reprinted in *SB* I). 1913. [Rp. AMH]

*XIV, *Die ältesten lateinischen und griechischen Papyri Wiens*, ed. C. Wessely. Nos. 1 and 2 are Greek, 3-14 Latin. 1914. [Rp. AMH]

XV, *Griechische und koptische Texte theologischen Inhalts* IV, ed. C. Wessely. Nos. 193-259. 1914. [Rp. AMH]

XVI, *Duodecim prophetarum minorum versionis Achmimicae Codex Rainerianus.* ed. C. Wessely. 1915. [Rp. AMH]

*XVII, Greek texts in: "Un document administratif du nome de Mendès," ed. V. Martin (pp.9-48); reedition by Martin of *P.Lond.* II 193 recto (pp.49-52); Indices to vols. XIII and XVII. 1917. [Rp. AMH]

XVIII, *Griechische und koptische Texte theologischen Inhalts* V, ed. C. Wessely. Nos. 260-290. 1917. [Rp. AMH]

XIX, *Studien zu den koptischen Rechtsurkunden aus Oberägypten*, ed. A. Steinwenter. 1920. [Rp. AMH]

*XX, *Catalogus Papyrorum Raineri. Series Graeca. Pars I. Textus Graeci papyrorum, qui in libro "Papyrus Erzherzog Rainer--Führer durch die Austellung Wien 1894" descripti sunt*, ed. C. Wessely. Nos. 1-308. 1921. [MF 2.118; rp. AMH]. This volume publishes the Greek text of all the papyri listed in the *Führer*; in pp.61-130 Wessely describes each papyrus and illustrates some, providing a commentary for the bare Greek texts published in *Stud.Pal.* XX. Many of the texts are republications of some first published in *CPR*. For a concordance see *BL Konkordanz* pp.56-58 and 251-256.

XXI, *Griechisch-ägyptischer Offenbarungszauber*, ed. Th. Hopfner. 1921. Revised ed. Amsterdam 1974. [Rp. AMH]

*XXII, *Catalogus papyrorum Raineri. Series Graeca. Pars II. Papyri N.24858-25024, aliique in Socnopaei Insula scripti*, ed. C. Wessely. Nos. 1-184. 1922. [MF 2.119; rp. AMH]

XXIII, *Griechisch-ägyptischer Offenbarungszauber: seine Methoden*, ed. Th. Hopfner. 1924. Revised ed. 1983-1990. [Rp. AMH]

Studi e Testi di Papirologia, published by the Istituto Papirologico "G. Vitelli". Florence 1966- .

1, *Il testamento romano attraverso la prassi documentale* I. *Le forme classiche di testamento*, by M. Amelotti. 1966.

2, *Ricerche sulla maiuscola biblica*, by G. Cavallo. 2 vols. 1967.

3, see Naldini (III, Corpora)

Tyche Suppl. = *Tyche*, Supplementbände. Vienna 1992- .

I, *A Mithraic Catechism from Egypt*, by W.M. Brashear. 1992. [o.e. AHN]

VI. PERIODICALS

Although individual and small groups of papyri occasionally receive their first or revised edition in any of numerous journals concerned more broadly with classical studies, a list is given here of those journals expressly embracing the publication of papyrological texts.

A. Journals Published Currently

Aegyptus = *Aegyptus, Rivista italiana di egittologia e papirologia.* Published semiannually by the Scuola di Papirologia dell'Università Cattolica del Sacro Cuore, Milano, 1920- . [o.e. VP]

AnalPap = *Analecta Papyrologica, Rivista di Studi Papirologici.* Pulished annually by the Facoltà di Lettere dell'Università di Messina, 1989- . [o.e. ES]

Archiv = *Archiv für Papyrusforschung und verwandte Gebiete.* Published annually by BSB B.G. Teubner Verlagsgesellschaft, Leipzig, 1901- . [o.e. ZA]

BASP = *The Bulletin of the American Society of Papyrologists.* Published quarterly by the Society, 1963- . [o.e. SP]

BASP Suppl.: see under Section V, Series.

BullCPS = *Bulletin of the Center of Papyrological Studies,* published annually by Ain Shams University, Cairo, 1985- .

Cd'É = *Chronique d'Égypte, Bulletin périodique de la Fondation Égyptologique Reine Élisabeth.* Published semiannually by the Fondation, Parc du Cinquantenaire 10, 1040 Bruxelles, 1925- . [o.e. FERE]

CRIPEL = *Cahiers de Recherches de l'Institut de Papyrologie et d'Égyptologie de Lille.* Lille and Paris 1973- .

I, *Etudes sur l'Egypte et le Soudan anciens.* Lille and Paris (Editions Universitaires) 1973.

II, *idem.* 1974.

III, *idem.* 1975.

IV, *idem.* Lille (Publications de l'Université de Lille III) n.d. (1976).

V, *idem*. n.d. (1979).

VI, *idem*. Lille (Presses Universitaires de Lille) 1981.

VII, *Sociétés urbaines en Égypte et au Soudan*. Lille (Presses Universitaires de Lille) 1985.

VIII, *idem*. 1986.

IX, *idem*. 1987.

X, *idem*. 1988.

XI, *idem*. Lille (Institut de Papyrologie et d'Egyptologie, Université Charles de Gaulle, Lille III) 1989.

XII, *idem*. 1990.

JJurPap = *The Journal of Juristic Papyrology*. Published by the Institute of Papyrology and Ancient Law, University of Warsaw, 1946- .

Pap.Lup. = *Papyrologica Lupiensia*. Published annually by the Dipartimento di Filologia Classica e Medioevale, Università degli Studi di Lecce, 1992- .

1, *Papiri letterari greci e latini*, ed. M. Capasso, 1992.

Tyche = *Tyche, Beiträge zur Alten Geschichte Papyrologie und Epigraphik*. Published annually for the Institut für Alte Geschichte, Universität Wien by Verlag Adolf Holzhausens, Vienna, 1986- .

ZPE = *Zeitschrift für Papyrologie und Epigraphik*. Published currently in four or five issues a year by Dr. Rudolf Habelt, Bonn, 1967- . Separate indices for vols. 1-30 (1978), 31-50 (1983), 51-75 (1989). [o.e. RH]

B. Discontinued Journals

Anagennesis = *Anagennesis, a Papyrological Journal*. Published semiannually by F.Farid†, Athens, 1981-1986 (vols. I-IV). Cf. P.Anag.

ÉdP = *Études de Papyrologie*. Published by the Société Égyptienne de Papyrologie, Cairo, 1932-1974 (vols. I-IX).

Mizraim = *Mizraim, Journal of Papyrology, Egyptology, History of Ancient Laws, and their Relations to the Civilizations of Bible Lands*. Published by Stechert, New York, 1933-1938 (vols. I-IX).

RechPap = *Recherches de Papyrologie*. Published by the Institut de Papyrologie de Paris, 1961-1967 (vols. I-IV).

Studî = *Studî della Scuola Papirologica*. Published by the Accademia Scientifico-Letteraria in Milano, 1915-1926 (vols. I-IV). [Rp. CG]

StudPap = *Studia Papyrologica, Rivista española de papirología.*
Published semiannually by Facultades de Filosofía y Teología,
San Cugat del Vallés, Barcelona, 1962-1983 (vols. I-XXII).

VII. INFORMATION ON PUBLISHERS

The publishers whose initials are given in the *Checklist* are listed below in the alphabetical order of the initials used. The addresses given are valid to the best of our current information but are, of course, subject to subsequent change.

MF = Microfiche edition in "Papyrology on Microfiche," published by the American Society of Papyrologists through Scholars Press; to order, write Scholars Press Customer Services, c/o Professional Book Distributors, P.O. Box 6996, Alpharetta, GA 30239-6996, U.S.A. The number after MF indicates the series and item number.

o.e. = Original edition or reprint by original publisher.

Rp. = Reprint.

AB	Academic Bookstore, P.O. Box 10128, Helsinki 10, Finland
AG	Dott. A. Giuffrè, Via Colonna 40, 00193 Roma, Italy
AHN	Verlag Adolf Holzhausens Nfg., Kandlgasse 19-21, 1070 Wien, Austria
AMH	Adolf M. Hakkert, Calle Alfambra 26, 35010 Las Palmas de Gran Canaria, Spain
AP	Ars Polona, Krakowskie Przedmiescie 7, Warsaw, Poland; distrib. Hippocrene Books, Inc., 171 Madison Ave., New York, NY 10016, U.S.A.
APS	American Philosophical Society, 104 South Fifth St., P.O. Box 40098, Philadelphia, PA 19106, U.S.A.
APU	Association des Publications près des Universités de Strasbourg, Universités des Sciences Humaines, 22 rue Descartes, 67084 Strasbourg, France
ARB	Académie Royale de Belgique, Palais des Académies, rue Ducale, 1000 Bruxelles, Belgium
ARES	ARES Publishers Inc., 7020 North Western Ave., Chicago, IL 60645, U.S.A.
AUP	Aberdeen University Press, Farmers Hall, Aberdeen, AB9 2XT, Scotland, U.K. for Scottish orders; for orders from

elsewhere, Pergamon Press PLC, Headlington Hill Hall, Oxford OX3 0BW, U.K.

AV   Akademie-Verlag GmbH, Leipziger Str. 3-4, Postfach 1233, O-1086 Berlin, Germany

AW   Almqvist & Wiksell International, Drottninggatan 108, P.O. Box 45150, 104-30 Stockholm, Sweden

BAM   Aegyptisches Museum, Schlossstr. 70, 1000 Berlin 19, Germany

BB   Bibliotheca Bodmeriana, 19-21 route de Guigrad, 1223 Cologny-Genève, Switzerland

Bd'E   Bottega d'Erasmo, Via Gaudenzio-Ferrari 9, 10124 Torino, Italy

BMP   British Museum Press, 30 Bloomsbury St., London WC1B 3QP, U.K.: distributed by Thames & Hudson Ltd, 44 Clockhouse Rd., Farnborough, Hants. GU14 7Q2, U.K.

BNU   Bibliothèque Nationale et Universitaire, 3 Ave. du Maréchal Joffre, BP 1029, 67070 Strasbourg, France

Brepols   N.V. Brepols, Baron Fr. du Fourstraat 8, 2300 Turnhout, Belgium

BTS   B.G. Teubner GmbH, Postfach 801069, 7000 Stuttgart, Germany

CG   Cisalpino Istituto Editoriale Universitario, Via Rezia 4, 20135 Milano, Italy

CUI   Institut for Graesk og Latinsk Middelalderfilologi, Njalsgade 94, 2300 Copenhagen, Denmark

CWV   Carl Winter Universitätsverlag, Lutherstrasse 59, Postfach 106140, 6900 Heidelberg, Germany

EES   Egypt Exploration Society, 3 Doughty Mews, London WC1N 2PG, England. Order from The Distribution Centre, Blackhorse Road, Letchworth, Hertfordshire SG6 1HN, England

EH   Dr. Ernst Hauswedell & Co., Rosenbergstrasse 113, Postfach 40155, 7000 Stuttgart 1, Germany

EJB   E.J. Brill, P.O. Box 9000, 2300 PA Leiden, Netherlands; in Germany, Antwerpenstrasse 6-12, 5000 Köln, Germany; in North America, 24 Hudson St., P.O. Box 467, Kinderhook, NY 12106, U.S.A.

ES   Editrice Sicania, Via Catania 62, 98124 Messina, Italy

FERE	Fondation Égyptologique Reine Élisabeth, Parc du Cinquantenaire 10, 1040 Bruxelles, Belgium
FLM	Casa Editrice Felice Le Monnier, Via Meucci 2, 50015 Grassina (Firenze), Italy
GB	Casa Editrice Giunti Barbera, Via Gioberti 34, 50121 Firenze, Italy
GO	Georg Olms Verlag GmbH, Hagentorwall 7, 3200 Hildesheim, Germany
GP	Greenwood Press, Inc., 88 Post Rd., W., Box 5007, Westport, CT 06881
GRBS	Greek, Roman, and Byzantine Studies, Box 4715 Duke Station, Durham, NC 27706, U.S.A.
HF	Hodges, Figgis & Co., The Mall, Donnybrook, Dublin 4, Ireland
HUP	Harvard University Press, 79 Garden St., Cambridge, MA 02138, U.S.A.
ICS	Institute of Classical Studies, Publications Dept., University of London, 31-34 Gordon Square, London WC1H 0PY, U.K.
JCG	J.C. Gieben, Nieuwe Herengracht 35, 1011 RM Amsterdam, Netherlands
JRL	John Rylands University Library of Manchester, Oxford Road, Manchester MI3 9PD, U.K.
LGF	Luigi Gonnelli e Figli, Via Ricasoli 14r, 50122 Firenze, Italy
NYU	New York University Press, 70 Washington Square South, New York, NY 10012
OH	Otto Harrassowitz, Taunusstrasse 5, Postfach 2929, 6200 Wiesbaden, Germany
ÖNB	Oesterreichische Nationalbibliothek, Josefsplatz 1, 1015 Wien, Austria
OUP	Oxford University Press, 200 Madison Ave., New York, NY 10016, U.S.A.
OZ	Otto Zeller Verlagsbuchhandlung GmbH, Jahnstr. 15, Postfach 1949, 4500 Osnabrück, Germany
PIB	Press of the Pontificio Istituto Biblico, Piazza della Pilotta 35, 00187 Roma, Italy
PUF	Presses Universitaires de France, 108 Blvd. Saint-Germain, 75006 Paris, France

PUP	Princeton University Press, 3175 Princeton Ave., Lawrenceville, NJ 08648, U.S.A.
PvZ	Verlag Philipp von Zabern, Welschnonnongasse 13A, Postfach 4065, 6500 Mainz am Rhein, Germany
RH	Dr. Rudolf Habelt, Am Buchenhang 1, Postfach 150104, 5300 Bonn 1, Germany
RHR	Rudolf H. Rohrer, Wassergasse 1, 2500 Baden, Austria
SEVPO	S.E.V.P.O., 2 rue Pau-Hervieu, 75015 Paris, France
SP	Scholars Press, P.O. Box 15288, Atlanta, GA 30333, U.S.A. For book orders, Scholars Press Customer Services, P.O. Box 6996, Alpharetta, GA 30239-6996 U.S.A.
TPC	Terra Publishing Company, P.O. Box 188, Zutphen, Netherlands
UF	Universitetsforlaget, Kolstadgt. 1, 0608 Oslo 6, Norway; distribut. Postboks 2977 Toyen, 0608 Oslo 6, Norway; in U.S.A., Columbia University Press, 136 South Broadway, Irvington on Hudson, NY 10533, U.S.A.
UGV	Urs Graf Verlag GmbH, Hasenbergstrasse 7, Postfach 66, 8953 Dietikon-Zürich, Switzerland
UTP	University of Toronto Press, Suite 700, 10 St. Mary's St., Toronto, Toronto, Ont. M4Y 2W8, Canada
UUB	Uppsala Universitetsbibliotek, Dag Hammarskjölds väg 1, Box 510, 751-20 Uppsala, Sweden
V&R	Vandenhoeck & Ruprecht, Theaterstraße 13, Postfach 3753, 3400 Göttingen, Germany
VAT	Biblioteca Apostolica Vaticana, Piazzale del Belvedere, 0012 Città del Vaticano (Roma), Italy
VP	Vita e Pensiero, Largo A. Gemelli 1, 20123 Milano, Italy
WdG	Walter de Gruyter, Genthiner Str. 13, Postfach 110240, 1000 Berlin 30, Germany
WDV	Westdeutscher Verlag GmbH, Faulbrunnenstr. 13, Postfach 5829, 6200 Wiesbaden 1, Germany
WHA	William H. Allen, Bookseller, 2031 Walnut St., Philadelphia, PA 19103, U.S.A.
ZA	Zentralantiquariat, Talstr. 29, Postfach 1080, 7010 Leipzig, Germany

VIII. LIST OF EDITIONS OF DOCUMENTARY PAPYRI BY YEAR OF PUBLICATION

Since this list is intended to facilitate research on documentary papyri, publications dealing exclusively with literary papyri have been omitted. Editions before 1891 are omitted as superseded. If indices to a certain publication followed in a later volume of the same series, or if indices are lacking thus far, the abbreviation is put between parentheses ( ). The reference has been repeated under the year of publication of the volume which contains the indices, e.g. 1901: (*Stud.Pal.* I); 1902: (*Stud.Pal.* II); 1905: *Stud.Pal.* (I + II +)IV. The dates of publication of fascicles of a volume are not taken into account, but those of separate parts are.

1891 *P.Petr.* I
1892 -
1893 *P.Lond.* I; *P.Petr.* II
1894 -
1895 *BGU* I; *CPR* I
1896 *P.Grenf.* I; *P.Rev.* 1st ed.
1897 *P.Grenf.* II
1898 *BGU* II; *P.Lond.* II; *P.Oxy.* I
1899 *P.Oxy.* II; *O.Wilck.*
1900 *P.Fay.*
1901 *P.Amh.* II; (*Stud.Pal.* I)
1902 *P.Cair.Goodsp.*; *P.Kar.Goodsp.*; *P.Tebt.* I; (*Stud.Pal.* II)
1903 *BGU* III; *P.Cair.Cat.*; *P.Oxy.* III
1904 *P.Oxy.* IV; (*Stud.Pal.* III)
1905 *P.Petr.* III; *P.Rein.* I; *Stud.Pal.* (I + II +)IV, V
1906 (*P.Catt.* I); *P.Flor.* I; *P.Gen.* I; *P.Hib.* I; *P.Lips.*; *P.Schott-Reinh.*
1907 *P.Eleph.*; *P.Lond.* III; *P.Tebt.* II
1908 *P.Flor.* II; *P.Oxy.* VI; *Stud.Pal.* VII, (III +)VIII
1909 -
1910 (*P.Giss.* I.1, I.2), *P.Lond.* IV; *P.Oxy.* VII; *Stud.Pal.* X
1911 *P.Cair.Masp.* I; *P.Cair.Preis.*; *P.Flor.* II; (*P.Hamb.* I.1); *P.Oxy.* VIII; *P.Thead.*

1912 *BGU* IV; (*P.Giss.* I.1-2+) I.3; *P.Lille* II; *P.Oxy.* IX; *PSI* I; *P.Stras.* I; *Chrest.Mitt.*; *Chrest.Wilck.*

1913 *P.Cair.Masp.* II; *P.Hal.*; (*P.Hamb.* I.2); (*P.Iand.* II, *P.Iand.* III); *Stud.Pal.* XIII; *O.Erem.*; *O.Theb.*

1914 *P.Freib.* I; (*P.Grad.*); (*P.Iand.* IV); *P.Monac.*; *P.Oxy.* X; *PSI* III; (*Stud.Pal.* XIV); *O.Joach.*

1915 *P.Flor.* III; *P.Ryl.* II; (*SB* I)

1916 *P.Cair.Masp.* III; (*P.Freib.* II); *P.Meyer*; *P.Oxy.* XII; *O.Deiss.*

1917 *P.Bas.*; *P.Lond.* V; *PSI* IV; *PSI* V; *Stud.Pal.* XVII

1918 -

1919 *BGU* V.1

1920 *P.Frankf.*; *P.Oxy.* XIV; *PSI* VI; *P.Stras.* II

1921 *P.Gur.*; *Stud.Pal.* XX

1922 *BGU* VI; *Stud.Pal.* XXII; *SB* (I+)II; *O.Brüss.Berl.*; *O.Sarga*

1923 *P.Bad.* II; *O.Stras.*

1924 *P.Bad.* IV; *P.Berl.Thun.*; (*P.Giss.Univ.* I); *P.Hamb.* I; *P.Lond.* VI; *P.Oxy.* XVI

1925 *P.Cair.Zen.* I; *PSI* VII

1926 *BGU* VII; *P.Bour.*; *P.Cair.Zen.* II; *P.Corn.*; (*P.Jena*)

1927 *P.Freib.* III; *P.Oxy.* XVII; *P.Ross.Georg.* IV; *PSI* VIII; (*UPZ* I); *SB* III

1928 *P.Cair.Zen.* III; *P.Lille* I; (*P.Mil.* I.1)

1929 *P.Berl.Möller*; *P.Col.* I; *P.Got.*; *P.Ross.Georg.* II; *PSI* IX

1930 *P.Achm.*; *P.Ross.Georg.* III; (*O.Bodl.* I, *O.Ashm.*, *O.Camb.*, *O.Minor*, *O.Petr.*)

1931 *P.Berl.Frisk*; *P.Cair.Zen.* IV; *P.Enteux.*; (*P.Giss.Univ.* III); *P.Marm.*; *P.Mich.* I; *P.Oslo* II; *P.Princ.* I; *SB* IV

1932 *P.Berl.Leihg.* I; *P.Col.* II; *PSI* X

1933 *BGU* VIII; *P.Gron.*; *P.Mich.* II; (*P.Princ.Roll*); (*P.Tebt.* III.1); *O.Oslo*

1934 *P.Col.* III; (*P.Iand.* VI, *P.Iand.* VII); *P.Würzb.*; *O.Buch.*

1935 *P.Ross.Georg.* V; *P.Vars.*; *O.Mich.* I; *O.Wilb.*

1936 *P.Brem.*; *P.Harr.* I; *P.Mich.* III; (*P.Mich.* IV.1); *P.Oslo* III; *P.Princ.* II

1937 *BGU* IX; *P.Edfou* I; *P.Mil.Vogl.* I; (*P.Lund* II): *O.Edfou* I

1938 *P.Bad.* VI; *P.Edfou* II; (*P.Iand.* VIII); (*P.Lund* III); *P.Tebt.* (III.1+)III.2; *O.Edfou* II

1939 *P.Aberd.*; *P.Adl.*; *P.Athen.*; *P.Fouad*; (*P.Giss.Univ.* VI); *P.Mich.* (IV.1+)IV.2

1940 *P.Cair.Zen.* V; *P.Col.* IV; *P.Rein.* II

1941 *P.Berl.Zill.*; *P.Oxy.* XVIII; *P.Warr.*

1942 *P.Erl.*; *P.Haun.* I; *P.Oxf.*; *P.Princ.* III; *P.Vind.Bosw.*

1943 -

1944 *P.Mich.* V; *P.Mich.* VI, *O.Mich.* II

1945 -

1946 (*P.Lund* IV); (*P.Prag.Varcl* I)

1947 *P.Bacch.*; *P.Lund* (II + III + IV +)V; *P.Mich.* VII (Latin); *P.Phil.*;
     (*P.Prag.Varcl* II)

1948 *P.Mert.* I; *P.Oxy.* XIX; (*P.Stras.* III)

1949 *P.Fuad I Univ.*

1950 *P.Ant.* I; *P.Edfou* III; *P.Fam.Tebt.*; *O.Edfou* III

1951 *P.Mich.* VIII, *O.Mich.* III; *PSI* XII

1952 (*P.Lund* VI); *P.Oxy.* XX; *P.Ryl.* IV; *SB* Bh. 1; *T.Alb.* (Latin)

1953 *P.Apoll.*; *P.Bon.* I; *PSI* XIII

1954 *P.Bal.*; *P.Col.* VI; *P.Hamb.* II; *P.Oxy.* XXII

1955 *P.Col.* VI 2nd ed.: *P.Hib.* II; *P.Ital.* I (Latin); *P.Michael.*; *SB* V;
     (*O.Bodl.* II)

1956 *P.Col.* V

1957 *P.Kroll*; *P.Oxy.* XXIV; (*P.Prag.Varcl* NS 1-3); *PSI* XIV; *UPZ* (I +)II;
     C.Pap.Jud. I

1958 *P.Heid.* II; *P.Ness.* III; (*P.Prag.Varcl* NS 4-10)

1959 *P.Dura*; *P.Mert.* II; (*P.Prag.Varcl* NS 11-21)

1960 *P.Ant.* II; *P.Cair.Isid.*; (*P.Prag.Varcl* NS 22-39); *C.Pap.Jud.* II

1961 (*P.Edfou* IX); *P.Mil.Vogl.* II; *P.Mur.* II; (*P.Prag.Varcl* NS 40-53);
     P.Sarap.; *SB* Bh. 2

1962 *P.Abinn.*; *P.Iand.inv.* 653; *P.Oxy.* XXVII

1963 *P.Heid.* III; *P.Leit.*; *P.Stras.* (III +)IV; *P.Vind.Sijp.*; (*SB* VI)

1964 *P.Alex.*; *P.Herm.*; *P.Panop.Beatty*; *SB* (VI +)VII; *O.Bodl.*
     (I + II +)III; (*C.Ord.Ptol.*); *C.Pap.Jud.* I + II + III

1965 *P.Mil.Vogl.* III; *P.Select.*; *PSI Congr.XI*

1966 *P.Mich.Mchl*; *P.Mil.* (I.1 +)II; *P.Oxy.* XXXI; *PSI* XV estr.; *P.Sorb.* I

1967 *P.Ant.* III; *P.Mert.* III; (*P.Mil.* I.1 2nd ed.); *P.Mil.Vogl.* IV; *P.NYU* I;
     P.Wisc. I; *P.Yale* I; (*SB* VIII)

1968 *BGU* XI; *P.David*; *P.Oxy.* XXXIII, XXXIV

1969 *P.Alex.Giss.*; *P.Petaus*; *SB* (VIII +)IX

1970 *BGU* X; *P.Mich.* X; *P.Oxy.* XXXVI

1971 (*P.IFAO* I, *P.IFAO* II); *P.Kron.*; *P.Mich.* IX; *P.Mich.* XI; *P.Oxy.*
     XXXVIII; (*P.Panop.* I + II); (*SB* X); *O.Ont.Mus.* I

1972 *P.Oxy.* XL; *P.Oxy.* XLI; *P.Vind.Worp*

1973 *P.Ashm.* I; *P.Berl.Brash.*; *P.Freer*, *P.Panop.* (I+II+)III; *P.Stras.* V; *SB* (X+)XI

1974 *BGU* XII; *P.Brux.* I; *P.Genova* I; *P.Lond.* VII; *P.Mil.Congr.XIV*; *P.Oxy.* XLII

1975 *P.Berl.Bork.*; (*P.Cair.Mich.* part 1); *P.Giss.Univ.* (I+III+VI) Indices; (*P.IFAO* III); *P.Mich.* XII; *P.Oxy.* XLIII; (*P.Stras.* VI); *O.Mich.* IV

1976 *BGU* XIII; *CPR* V; *P.Coll.Youtie* I+II; *P.Köln* I; *P.Laur.* I; *P.Oxy.* XLIV; *P.Tebt.* IV; *P.Theon.*; *P.Vind.Sal.*; *P.Vind.Tand.*; *O.Amst.*; *O.Florida*; *O.Medin.Madi*; *O.Ont.Mus.* II; *C.Étiq.Mom.*

1977 *P.Berl.Leihg.* II; *P.Cair.Mich.* (I+)II; *P.Laur.* II; *P.Mich.* XIII; *P.Mil.Vogl.* VI; *P.Oxy.* XLV; *PSI Corr.* I; *P.Tebt.Tait*; *P.Wisc.* II; (*SB* XII); *O.Brux.* 2nd ed.; *Pap.Biling.*

1978 (*CPR* VI,1); *P.Batav.* I; *P.Herm.Landl.*; *P.Hombert*; *P.Köln* II; *P.Oxy.* XLVI; *P.Sakaon*

1979 *CPR* VII; *P.Col.* VII; *P.Congr.XV*; *P.Laur.* III; *P.Oxy.Hels.*; *P.Soter.*; (*P.Stras.* VII); *SB* (XII+)XIII; *O.Lund*; *O.Tebt.Pad.*

1980 *P.Amst.* I; *BGU* XIV; *P.Charite*; *P.Genova* II; *P.Köln* III; *P.Mich.* XIV; *P.Oxy.* XLVII; *P.Panop.* (repr.); (*P.Stras.* VIII.701-720); *P.Vat.Aphrod.*; *P.Wash.Univ.* I; *P.Zen.Pestm.*; *O.Leid.*

1981 *P.Haun.* II; *P.Mil.Vogl.* VII; *P.Nag Hamm.*; *P.Oxy.* XLVIII; (*P.Stras.* VIII.721-740); *P.Tor.Amen.*; *P.Turner*, *P.Ups.Frid*; (*SB* XIV.1)

1982 *P.Dion.*; *P.Ital.* II (Latin); *P.Köln* IV; *P.Mich.* XV; *P.Oxy.* XLIX; (*P.Stras.* VIII.741-760)

1983 *BGU* XV; *CPR* VIII; *P.Laur.* IV; *P.Leeds Mus.*; *P.Mil.Congr.* XVII; *P.Oxy.* L; *P.Rain.Cent.*; *PSI Congr.XVII*; (*P.Stras.* VIII.761-780); *P.Tebt.Wall*; (*SB* XIV.2-3); *O.Cair.Cat.*; *T.Vindol.* (Latin)

1984 *CPR* IX; *P.Hamb.* III; *P.Oxy.* LI, LII; *P.Princ.Roll* 2nd ed.; (*P.Stras.* VIII.781-800); *C.Pap.Gr.* I

1985 (*CPR* VI.1+)VI.2; *P.Harr.* II; *P.Haun.* III; *P.Köln* V; (*P.Stras.* IX.801-820); *P.Thmouis* I; (*SB* XVI.1-2); *C.Pap.Gr.* II.1

1986 *CPR* X; *P.Anag.*; *P.Erasm.* I; *P.Freib.* IV; *P.Gen.* II; *P.Heid.* IV; *P.Hels.* I; *P.Münch.* I, III.1; *P.Mil.Congr.XVIII*; *P.Quseir*; (*P.Stras.* IX.821-840); *P.Stras.* (VI-VIII) Indices; *O.Cair.*; *O.Douch* I; *Pap.Agon.*

1987 *CPR* XIII; *P.Customs*; *P.Köln* VI; *P.Neph.*; *P.Oxy.* LIV; (*P.Stras.* IX.841-860); *O.Oasis*

1988 *P.Oxy.* LV; *P.Prag.* I; (*P.Stras.* IX.861-880); (*SB* XVI.3); *O.Ashm.Shelt.*; *O.Douch* II

1989 *CPR* XIV; *P.Babatha*; *P.Masada, O.Masada*; *P.Mil.Congr.* XIX;
      P.Oxy. LVI; (*P.Stras.* IX.881-900); *O.Elkab*; *T.Varie*
1990 *CPR* XV; *P.Bub.* I; *P.Col.* VIII; *P.Diog.*; *P.Heid.* V; *P.Matr.*; *P.Oxy.*
      LVII; *P.Wash.Univ.* II
1991 *CPR* XVIIA, XVIIB, XVIII; *P.Erasm.* II; *P.Genova* III; *P.Köln* VII;
      P.Leid.Inst.; *P.Oxy.* LVIII; *P.Petr.*[2] I
1992 *P.Brook.*; *PSI XX Congr.*; *P.Tor.Choach.*; *O.Claud.* I; *O.Douch* III

IX. PROCEEDINGS OF INTERNATIONAL CONGRESSES

I   "Semaine Égyptologique et Papyrologique du 14 au 20 septembre 1930." Brussels. Published in *Cd'É* 6 (1931) 189-470.

II   "XVIIIe Congrès International des Orientalistes. Leyde, du 7 au 12 septembre 1931. Section Autonome des Papyrologues." Published in *Cd'É* 7 (1932) 127-348.

III *Papyri und Altertumswissenschaft. Vorträge des 3. Internationalen Papyrologentages in München vom 4. bis 7. September 1933.* (Münchener Beiträge zur Papyrusforschung und antiken Rechtsgeschichte 19, Munich 1934).

IV   *Atti del IV Congresso Internazionale di Papirologia, Firenze, 28 aprile-2 maggio 1935.* (*Aegyptus*, Serie scientifica 5, Milan 1936).

V   *Actes du Ve Congrès International de Papyrologie, Oxford, 30 août-3 septembre 1937.* Published by the Fondation Égyptologique Reine Élisabeth. (Brussels 1938).

VI   Paris, 29 August-4 September 1949. No proceedings published.

VII *L'Originalité de l'Égypte dans le monde gréco-romain, Septième Congrès International de Papyrologie, Genève, 1-6 septembre 1952. Museum Helveticum* 10 (1953) 129-180.

VIII *Akten des VIII. Internationalen Kongresses für Papyrologie, Wien 1955.* (29 August-3 September). (*MPER* N.S. V, Vienna 1956).

IX   *Proceedings of the IX International Congress of Papyrology, Oslo, 19-22 August 1958.* Published by the Norwegian Research Council for Science and the Humanities (Oslo 1961).

X   *Actes du Xe Congrès International de Papyrologie, Varsovie-Cracovie, 3-9 septembre 1961.* Published by the Comité des Sciences de la Culture Antique, Académie Polonaise des Sciences. (Warsaw 1964).

XI   *Atti dell'XI Congresso Internazionale di Papirologia, Milano, 2-8 settembre 1965.* Published by the Istituto Lombardo di Scienze e Lettere. (Milan 1966).

XII *Proceedings of the Twelfth International Congress of Papyrology, Ann Arbor, 13-17 August 1968.* (Am.Stud.Pap. VII, Toronto 1970).

XIII *Akten des XIII. Internationalen Papyrologenkongresses, Marburg/Lahn, 2-6 August 1971.* (Münchener Beiträge zur

Papyrusforschung und antiken Rechtsgeschichte 66, Munich 1974).

XIV *Proceedings of the XIV International Congress of Papyrologists, Oxford, 24-31 July 1974.* (Egypt Exploration Society, Graeco-Roman Memoirs 61, London 1975).

XV *Actes du XVe Congrès International de Papyrologie, Brussels, 29 August-3 September 1977.* (Pap.Brux. XVI-XIX, Brussels 1978).

XVI *Proceedings of the Sixteenth International Congress of Papyrology New York, 24-31 July 1980.* (Am.Stud.Pap. XXIII, Chico 1981).

XVII *Atti del XVII Congresso Internazionale di Papirologia.* 3 vols. (Centro Internazionale per lo Studio dei Papiri Ercolanesi, Naples 1984).

XVIII *Proceedings of the XVIII International Congress of Papyrology, Athens 25-31 May 1986*, ed. B. Mandilaras. 2 vols. (Greek Papyrological Society, Athens 1988).

XIX *Proceedings of the XIXth International Congress of Papyrology, Cairo 2-9 September 1989*, ed. A.H.S. El-Mosallamy. 2 vols. (Ain Shams University, Center of Papyrological Studies, Cairo 1992)

There is an index to the papers in the Congress volumes of Congresses I through XIII prepared by K.A. Worp and published in *Museum Philologicum Londinense* II (1977) 283-305.

APPENDIX

OTHER CITATIONS SOMETIMES USED FOR EDITIONS OF PAPYRI

The following list is not at this time meant to be exhaustive; it contains abbreviations we are aware of and which might be difficult to decipher or are of such age as to be no longer in current use. Our aim is to direct users to the full bibliographical information in the lists of editions.

Apokrimata: see *P.Col.* VI
Chrest.: see *Chrest.Mitt./Chrest.Wilck.* (III, Corpora)
C.P.An.: see *P.Anag.*
C.P.Herm. = *Corpus Papyrorum Hermopolitanarum*: see *Stud.Pal.* V (V, Series)
Dikaiomata: see *P.Hal.*
DJD: see *P.Mur.*
Führer PER, PERF: see *Papyrus Erzherzog Rainer. Führer durch die Ausstellung*, Vienna 1892, 1894 (2nd edition); many of the texts are published in full in *Stud.Pal.* XX (V, Series).
Gradenwitz, *Erbstreit*: see *SB* I 4512
G.S.M.: see *Shorthand Manuals* (III, Corpora)
Heid.Veröff.: see *P.Heid.*
Mon.Epiph.: For Greek texts see *SB* IV 7477-7514
Negotia: see *FIRA* III (III, Corpora)
O.Brüss.Berl.: see *O.Berl.* and *O.Brux.*
O.Cair.: see also *O.Cair.Cat.*
O.Cair.GPW: see *O.Cair.*
O.Leiden Insinger: see *O.Leid.*
O.Tait: see *O.Bodl.*
O.Viereck: see *O.Stras.*
O.Zereteli: see *O.Erem.*
P.Amst.: see also *P.Gron.*
P.Amstel.: see *P.Gron.Amst.*
P.Aphrodito: see *Grundz.Wilck.* xxv for various editions

P.Arsinoe: see *P.Haw.*
P.Artemisia: text in *SB* I 5103, *UPZ* I 1
P.Ashmol.: see *P.Ashm.*
P.Athen.S.A.: see *P.Athen.*
P.Ausonia: texts now in *P.Flor.* III 291, 357, 358
P.Bakchiastexte: see *P.Lund* IV
P.Bankakten: see *P.Berl.Frisk*
PBeatty Panop.: see *P.Panop.Beatty*
P.Beaugé: texts in *P.Cair.Masp.* II 67156, III 67279, 67305
P.Bibl.Univ.Giss.: see *P.Giss.Univ.*
P.Boissier: text now *Chrest.Wilck.* 13
P.Buttmann: text in *UPZ* II 175b
P.Cair.: see *P.Cair.Cat.*
P.Cair.Byz.: see *P.Cair.Masp.*
P.Cair. GH: see *P.Cair.Cat.*
P.Casati: see *UPZ* II 180a
P.Catt.: see *Chrest.Mitt.* 88 and 372 for No. I and *SB* I 4284 for No. II.
P.Ceriani: see *UPZ* I 46
P.Chester Beatty: see *P.Beatty*
P.Chic.Goodsp.: see *P.Kar.Goodsp.*
P.Col.123: see *P.Col.* VI
P.Col.480: see *P.Col.* I
P.Col.Zen.: see *P.Col.* III and IV
P.Colon.: see *P.Köln*
P.Colon.Panop.: see *P.Panop.*
P.Colt: see *P.Ness.*
P.Cong.Omaggio: see *PSI Cong.XI*
P.Copenhagen: text now in *SB* I 428; see also *P.Haun.*
P.Denkschriften: see the listing in *SB* II pp.74-82
P.Didot: text now in *UPZ* I 56
P.Dresden: texts now in *UPZ* I 34, 43, 44
P.Droysen: texts now in *UPZ* II passim
P.Edmondstone: see *BASP* 15 (1978) 235-36
P.Eitrem: See listing in *SB* II, p.83
P.Feste: see *Feste* (III, Corpora)
P.Fuad: see also *P.Fouad*
P.Fraser: text now in *UPZ* I 158b,c
P.Frisk: see *P.Berl.Frisk*

P.Gentili: texts now *SB* I 5658, *P.Flor.* III 368-370

P.Germ.: text now *SB* I 3924

P.Gnomon: see *BGU* V

P.Goodsp.: see *P.Cair.Goodsp.*, *P.Chic.* and *P.Kar.Goodsp.*

P.Graux: texts now *SB* IV 7461-68

P.Graz: texts now in *Stud.Pal.* IV pp. 114-21, *P.Turner* 50, and *SB* XVI 12484

P.Grey: texts now in *UPZ* II 165-67

P.Gr.Texte: see *P.Meyer*

P.Ham.: see *JJurPap* 13 (1961) 33-51

P.Heid. 1280: text now *SB* I 4638

P.Hernals: see listing in *SB* II p.93

P.Hess.: see *P.Giss.*

P.Ibscher: see *P.Hamb.* II and Montevecchi, *La Papirologia* p.418

P.Innsbruck: text in *UPZ* I 136

P.Jand.: see *P.Iand.*

P.Jernstedt: text now *Chrest.Wilck.* 155

P.Jews: see *P.Lond.* VI

P.Jomard: text in *P.Paris* p.257

P.Jud.Des.: see *P.Mur.*

P.Karanis: see *P.Kar.Goodsp.*

P.Kl.Form.: see *Stud.Pal.* III and VIII (V, Series)

P.Köln Panop.: see *P.Panop.*

P.Landlisten: see *P.Herm.Landl.*

P.Lewald: see *P.Frankf.*

P.Libbey: text in *SB* I 2051

P.Libelli: see for listing *SB* II p.140

P.Lit.Lond.: see *P.Lond.Lit.*

P.Louvre: see *UPZ* passim; cf. also *P.Denkschriften*, above in this list

P.Lugd.Bat.: see *P.Batav.*, *P.David*, *P.Leid.*, *P.Leid.Inst.*; *P.L.Bat.* and *Pap.Lugd.Bat.* (V, Series)

P.Magd.: see *P.Lille* II

P.Magirus: texts now in *SB* I 5317-40

P.Maspero: see *P.Cair.Masp.*

P.Med.: see *P.Mil.*

P.Mel.Rev.: see the listing in *SB* II p.140 under Revillout, *Mélanges*

P.Mich.Browne: see *P.Mich.* X

P.Mich.Shelton: see *P.Mich.* XI

P.Mich.Sokn.Nes.: texts now *SB* V 7818-32

P.Mich.Zen.: see *P.Mich.* I

P.Milit.: see *Rom.Mil.Rec.* (III, Corpora)

P.Mimaut: text now *Pap.Graec.Mag.* I 3

P.Minutoli: see *UPZ* II 181

P.Mitt.PER, P.Mitt.Rain., P.Mitteilungen Wien: see *MPER* (V, Series)

P.Möller: see *P.Berl.Möller*

P.Mon., P.Mun.: see *P.Monac.* and *P.Münch.*

P.Neutest.: see *P.Meyer*

P.New York: see *UPZ* I 132,134; *P.NYU*

P.Panop.Borkowski: see *P.Berl.Bork.*

P.Papyrus Roll: see *P.Princ.Roll*

P.Passalacqua: see *UPZ* II 159

P.Petersb.: texts now in *P.Ross.Georg.* (I 22; III 26; V 5, 19, 56)

P.PRIMI: see *P.Mil.Vogl.* I

P.Real.Ist.Veneto: texts now in *P.Flor.* III 280, 283, 286

P.Rend.Harr.: see *P.Harr.*

PRG: see *P.Ross.Georg.*

PRUM: see *P.Mil.Vogl.* I

P.SAA, P.S.A.Athens: see *P.Athen.*

P.Sachini, Sakkinis, Sakkakinis: text now in *UPZ* II 158a

P.Salt.: text now in *UPZ* II 188

P.Schmidt: see *P.Berl.Schmidt*

P.Schott-Reinh.: see *P.Heid.* III

P.Sitol.: see *P.Berl.Thun.*

P.Soc., P.Soc.Ital.: see *PSI*

P.Socnobr.: see *P.Bacch.*

P.Stud.: see *Stud.Pal.* (V, Series)

PSI Omaggio: see *PSI Congr.XI*

PTA: see *Pap.Texte Abh.* (V, Series)

P.Taxroll: see *P.Princ.Roll*

P.Testa: see *SB* I 4505, 5285-86

P.Theb.Bank: see *Actenstücke*

P.Tiberii Julii Theones: see *P.Theon.*

P.Top.Äg.: see *Stud.Pal.* X (V, Series)

P.Tsoukalas: see *P.Athen.*

PUG: see *P.Genova*

P.Variae: see *P.Alex.Giss.*

P.Vat.: texts now in *UPZ* passim

P.Vat. II, P.Vat.gr. 11: see *P.Marm.*
P.Weil: text now in *UPZ* I 56
P.Wessely Prag.: see *P.Prag.*
P.Yadin: see *P.Babatha*
P.Zereteli: see *P.Ross.Georg.* passim
P.Zois: text now in *UPZ* I 114
V.B.P.: see *P.Bad.*
V.H.P.: see *P.Heid.*